The Prudent Investor's Guide to Beating Wall Street at Its Own Game

Second Edition

John J. Bowen, Jr.

Daniel C. Goldie

McGraw-Hill

New York   San Francisco   Washington, D.C.   Auckland   Bogotá
Caracas   Lisbon   London   Madrid   Mexico City   Milan
Montreal   New Delhi   San Juan   Singapore
Sydney   Tokyo   Toronto

Library of Congress Cataloging-in-Publication Data

Bowen, John J.
      The prudent investor's guide to beating Wall Street at its own game
—2nd ed. / John Bowen, Dan Goldie.
          p.   cm.
      Includes bibliographical references and index.
      ISBN 0-07-052760-1
      1. Investments—Handbooks, manuals, etc.   I. Title.
HG4527.B63   1998
332.6—dc21   98-6270
                                                              CIP

McGraw-Hill

*A Division of The **McGraw·Hill** Companies*

    2 3 4 5 6 7 8 9 0 DOC/DOC 9 0 3 2 1 0 9 8

ISBN 0-07-052760-1

*The sponsoring editor for this book was Stephen Isaacs, the editing supervisor was
John M. Morriss, and the production supervisor was Suzanne W. B. Rapcavage. It was set
in Palatino by Inkwell Publishing Services.*

Printed and bound by R.R. Donnelly & Sons Company.

This publication is designed to provide accurate and authoritative information in regard to
the subject matter covered. It is sold with the understanding that neither the author nor the
publisher is engaged in rendering legal, accounting, or other professional service. If legal
advice or other expert assistance is required, the services of a competent professional person should be sought.

> *—From a declaration of Principles jointly adopted by a Committee of
> the American Bar Association and a Committee of Publishers.*

McGraw-Hill books are available at special quantity discounts to use as premiums and sales
promotions, or for use in corporate training programs. For more information, please write
to the Director of Special Sales, McGraw-Hill, 11 West 19th Street, New York, NY 10011. Or
contact your local bookstore.

Contents

3 CHAPTER

From Noise to Information   27

4 CHAPTER

Effective Diversification Reduces Risk and Enhances Return   43

5 CHAPTER

The Role of Size and Value   59

APPENDIX

Formulas   *169*

Index   *175*

Foreword

There's probably only one kind of investing that really works for the average investor: It's called asset class investing. You have probably never heard of it. That's why we've written this book. We want to spread the ideas of asset class investing to as many people as we can.

This book will teach you the principles of asset class investing and how you can use it to beat Wall Street at its own game. It will dramatically change the way you think about how the stock market works and how you should invest your own hard-earned money. In fact, the ideas of asset class investing are so compelling that you will probably never want to invest any other way.

Asset class investing is a method of managing money that is not new. Its concepts are well documented and time-tested. In fact, a French mathematician first published the academic ideas that created the foundation of asset class investing back in 1900. Over the last 40 years, literally dozens of major academic and professional studies have confirmed the validity of this early work.

Most of Wall Street is not thrilled with asset class investing. Why? Because asset class investing states firmly that traditional Wall Street investment strategies—primarily stock picking and market timing—do not work. They are costly for the investor and largely ineffective. Wall Street spends billions of dollars each year trying to deliver market-beating returns for their clients. But there is something that they don't want you to know: *Wall Street is not beating the market, the market is beating them.*

After you read this book you will take a very skeptical view of Wall Street's investment advice. Wall Street is not happy with us and others who claim that their services do not add value. But the fact is that investment consultants and academic researchers have been generating remarkably consistent data about the performance of professional money managers for decades, beginning in the 1950s when computers were first able to crunch large amounts of data.

What researchers have found is that the majority of professional money managers do not beat the market. Moreover, there is no consistency among the few top performers that are successful. The good, mediocre, and bad performers rotate about performance charts more or less at random, as if they are playing musical chairs. Top performers regress to the mean almost as soon as you can spot them. And managers with bad records will suddenly top the charts. You never know who will win or lose next, only that most will underperform market averages.

When we first became aware of these studies, they caused an intellectual metamorphosis in our firm that shook the very foundation of our beliefs about how markets work and how we should invest our clients' money. We will reveal to you, in this book, everything we have learned about why traditional investment strategies do not work. We will show how you can beat Wall Street at its own game simply by refusing to play. You will stand aside, with an almost Zen-like strategy, while everyone else battles it out. You will end up winning the game with a lot less effort and risk.

Today we are in the middle of a quantum leap forward in our ability to design portfolios to efficiently manage the risk of stock and bond investing. That's good news. This book, with the concepts it represents, is an outgrowth of an evolution in thought about how to manage risk and capture consistent long-term returns with asset class mutual funds.

Asset class investing is about taking advantage of the most current thinking available today and designing portfolios that use this knowledge successfully. It is a strategic, long-term investment philosophy that allows you to step into the world of rational thought and empirical evidence—and out of the world of emotional, senseless trading and market timing.

The tools and techniques available to investors have evolved dramatically within the last five years. Right now you can buy over 8,000 mutual funds. Electronic trading is taking off like a rocket. The investment information available for free over the Web is staggering. How do you make investment decisions with all the information and options available to you? Simple. This book shows you how asset class investing allows you to separate noise from information and focus on what really determines investment results. You won't be distracted by Wall Street's investment product of the day. You will stay focused and disciplined, and you will pay attention to what works.

This book tells you everything we know about prudent investing in a way that is easily understood and usable for the average investor who is serious about asset growth. If you are new to investing, don't worry. We will take you by the hand and walk you through these ideas step by step. If you are an experienced investor, you will find our ideas refreshing, exciting, and new. You will benefit from a new way of managing your money—a method that involves the best elements of diversification, prudence, and efficiency.

You are about to read some of the most exciting investment ideas to come along since Harry Markowitz pioneered and discovered Modern Portfolio Theory in the 1950s. These concepts will show you that the best way to lower risk and raise expected return is to invest in many asset classes rather than just a few, and in many markets, rather than in one. You will discover that there is nothing revolutionary about what you are going to read. It's all grounded in well documented academic research.

You will also learn why so many of today's commonly held beliefs about market behavior and investing are just plain wrong. Most are misguided and lack any theoretical foundation. Many of these false ideas are so widespread that you have accepted them without really thinking about whether they make sense. When you take a step back, consider all the facts, and engage your newly acquired knowledge of how markets work, the logical errors of these investment strategies become clear to you. The best part is that you will be able to properly evaluate investment advice you receive. You will never again fall prey to the misguided recommendation of an uninformed advisor or investor.

If you have a serious mindset about the future of your own money, strategically managed portfolios using asset class mutual funds is the only rational, intelligent approach to obtaining consistent long-term results. Think of this book as your investment survival guide. Read it and enjoy. Your financial life will never be the same. And remember, you *can* beat Wall Street at its own game!

JOHN BOWEN AND DAN GOLDIE

1

Introduction

If we could show you how you could make smart investment decisions without having to spend all day following the stock market, would you be willing to spend a few hours learning how?

America is a country formed out of a revolution of new ideas; we have always welcomed change. Right now an important revolution is taking place on Wall Street. It is affecting the way billions of dollars are invested around the world.

After reading this book you will be able to take advantage of these new ideas and invest more confidently. You will no longer feel the need to search every financial publication for the latest investment insights. You will know that the basis of your investment strategy has been prudently researched by some of the finest financial minds in the country. We believe you will find the investment concepts in this book refreshing and rewarding. If you really take the time to learn these concepts, they will change the way you think about investing and the markets, forever.

At first glance this book may look like every other book on investing. You may even have heard these same promises before. That's okay. We invite you to be skeptical; that's a good attitude to have as an investor. Nevertheless, we think investing can be easy and understandable—that's why we have written this book.

OUR STORY

In the 1980s, dramatic changes took place in the investment community. The number of investment products available to the public increased exponentially, while the quality diminished significantly. Those were very frustrating times for us.

As strategic partners in a successful financial planning firm, we work with thousands of individual investors. Our main goal has always been to help our clients reach their financial goals. As part of this process, we prepared elaborate financial plans for our clients that clearly mapped out the path to successful attainment of their financial goals, and implemented the plans with investments from outside providers. If the outside investments performed to their stated expectations, our clients would achieve their goals. However, in many cases the actual results were disappointing. We asked ourselves, "What good are our carefully prepared financial plans if the implementation vehicles do not perform as expected?"

This frustration caused us to search for a better solution. We knew there must be a better way to invest our clients' money than to use the strategies that Wall Street was touting. We spent five years looking for solutions.

During that time, we discovered a remarkable fact: The fastest-growing investment strategy among institutional investors was almost completely unavailable and unknown to individual investors. At the time, most of the advice being given to individuals had little to do with the principles of investment theory, and much of it did not make good economic sense. It was more marketing hype than prudent investment advice. Unfortunately, this is still often true today.

Our quest led us to some of the top academics in the field of financial economics. Their ideas and investment theories were backed up by mountains of research and proof, but only the very largest institutions were taking advantage of this knowledge. The concepts developed by three men in particular were so influential to the field of finance that the trio won the Nobel Prize in Economics in 1990. Their ideas are collectively known as Modern Portfolio Theory.

We realized that our clients would gain tremendous benefit if we could give them the same Nobel Prize-winning investment strategies that were currently being used by major institutions. Our clients would truly be on the right road to fulfilling their financial goals.

At first we weren't sure that individual investors would understand these concepts. Many in the academic community discouraged us from trying to communicate the ideas. They were used to working with other academics or with sophisticated investment committees of large pension plans. They felt the strategies involved would be too complicated for private investors, and would confuse them into inaction.

Nevertheless, we moved forward, communicating these profound investment ideas to our clients. We happily discovered that the logic of the ideas is so compelling, new, and refreshing that our clients were quick to grasp it. After all, in many cases they were investing their life savings with us, so they were very willing to spend time learning to understand the concepts and how markets really work. Amazingly, these strategies actually simplified the investment decision-making process and allowed our clients the freedom to focus on other parts of their lives. We found that once investors truly understood how markets work, they were more comfortable with their investments.

Today, we find that many investors are skeptical of the investment community in general. Some have been disappointed by a stockbroker or investment manager who had a convincing story about how an approach was going to "beat the market," but whose strategies ultimately were not successful. Other disappointed investors purchased "hot" mutual funds with great track records, only to watch them turn cold and deliver returns far short of expectations and market benchmarks.

Those results are not surprising to us. In fact, we wonder why there aren't more unhappy investors. Believe it or not, the vast majority of investment managers and mutual funds don't beat the simple buy-and-hold approach, and those that do are part of a randomly changing group that is only marginally successful. In short, most investment managers and mutual funds do not follow through on their promises: *They do not beat the market.*

This may sound hard to believe, but it is totally consistent with the ideas of modern finance. An efficiently functioning capital market immediately incorporates all information into securities prices. The market price of any publicly traded asset reflects the collective estimate of its value of all market participants.[1] An investment manager can only beat the market if he or she can consistently identify mispriced securities *and* take advantage of the mispricing after the costs of trading. Given the speed and size of information flow today, this seems unlikely. Historical evidence confirms how difficult it is, for professionals and amateurs alike, to beat the market.

Fortunately, there is an alternative. We call it asset class investing. The beauty of this strategy is that it works in harmony with market efficiency, rather than against it. Asset class investing as a strategy is consistent with the ideas of modern finance and is supported by decades of empirical evidence. After you read this book, you will fully understand the overwhelming logic and power of this approach.

We believe that asset class investing and other passive strategies will dramatically alter the way individuals invest their money in the future. We hope that this book will help these ideas become more popular with individual investors. We owe the financial security of our families to these concepts. We hope you will take advantage of them too.

---

[1]We are not suggesting that all market prices are "correct," only that they reflect all known information.

ASSET CLASS INVESTING: A DEFINITION

Asset class investing involves the construction of portfolios that reliably deliver the returns of a specific asset class—a group of securities that share common risk and return characteristics. An investor constructs this portfolio by purchasing all, or a large sample of, the securities within the asset category under consideration. No subjective forecasting of market or economic conditions is involved, and no attempt is made to distinguish between undervalued and overvalued securities. Securities are considered for purchase when they meet the asset class parameters defined by the investment manager; they are considered for sale when they do not.

WHO SHOULD READ THIS BOOK?

We have determined that there are basically three types of investors: conservative, aggressive, and prudent. People in the first group think the stock and bond markets are really casinos. To protect their principal, conservatives invest primarily in certificates of deposit (CDs) and money market funds. Those types of investments offer stability of principal. But with CD rates usually just keeping up with inflation, conservative investors need higher returns, without having to go out on a limb. Often, they know they cannot reach their goals with the low rates of return CDs offer, but they are uncomfortable about making any changes until they are sure they are doing the right thing. We will illustrate how conservative investors can balance their desire for low risk while satisfying their need for growth above the level of inflation.

The second type of investor wants aggressive growth. People in this group usually have brokerage accounts and call their own shots, often with the help of stockbrokers. Aggressive investors want double-digit returns. It seems they are always searching for the next hot investment or "investment guru." If aggressive investors make the wrong decisions, they'll get hammered; they'll be worse off than when they started. They intuitively know there must be a better way, but they are not sure what it is. Using our strategies, aggressive investors will have a higher likelihood of achieving their goals consistently over time, while experiencing substantially lower risk.

The third group of investors is the largest group, fitting somewhere in between the first two extremes. They're basically conservative and safety-conscious, but they want to earn a fair return on their investments. We call these people prudent investors. Prudent investors will benefit most from this book.

Prudent investors are willing to take some risk—if the returns are commensurate. They are often uncomfortable with investments because they do not understand how markets work. It's not that they aren't financially savvy; it's just that they have not been exposed to the basic concepts. Often they work with investment advisors, many of whom ask them to take a leap of faith. Unfortunately, you already know the all-to-frequent result. In this book, *we will not ask you to take a leap of faith*. We will document and justify all our conclusions. We will empower you to make the correct decisions for yourself or, if you wish, to choose an advisor who can implement these principles.

There is an intelligent approach to investing that will help all investors achieve their personal financial goals. The first step is to free your mind of all the self-serving investment advice you have received in the past, and learn about investing and how markets work.

THE BEGINNING OF ASSET CLASS INVESTING

It all started in March of 1952, when arguably the most famous insight in the history of modern investing was published. It appeared in the *Journal of Finance*; its author was an unknown 25-year-old graduate student named Harry Markowitz.[2] He is credited with forging a new way of looking at how we divide our assets so that we can minimize risk and maximize returns.

For years, Markowitz wrestled with a broad philosophical question: How can people make the best possible decisions when dealing with the inescapable tradeoffs in life? He knew that investors faced especially tough questions. How can one earn attractive returns without accepting undue amounts of risk? How much risk is it necessary to take to achieve one's goals?

Using mathematics to solve the puzzle, Markowitz discovered a remarkable new way to build an investment portfolio. He was guided by one assumption: He believed that it was possible to scientifically minimize risks and improve returns in a diversified portfolio.

Eventually Markowitz developed a mathematically optimal portfolio. Based on his study of historical investment performance, he re-created the best combination of securities in a portfolio. Markowitz called this mathematically correct portfolio an *efficient portfolio*. His method sought to achieve maximum returns with the least amount of risk. The scientific system that Markowitz pioneered came to be known as Modern Portfolio Theory.

The powerful investment strategies we present here work equally well for conservative, moderate, or aggressive investors. You can use in-

---

[2]Markowitz, Harry, "Portfolio Selection," *The Journal of Finance* (March, 1952), pp. 77-91.

vestment strategies based on Modern Portfolio Theory to build your own portfolio for retirement, to protect your assets once you've retired, or to meet other financial goals. Amazingly, these strategies actually simplify the investment decision-making process.

Markowitz first published the theoretical foundation for Modern Portfolio Theory over 45 years ago. Since then his ideas have been tested and refined. His strategies are now accepted worldwide as the authoritative blueprint for prudent investing—that is, wisely and cautiously providing for the future.

RETHINK ALL INVESTMENT ADVICE

In 1986, a prestigious pension fund consulting firm released a startling research report. The firm analyzed the performance variations of 91 large pension funds.[3] Their conclusions sent shock waves throughout the investment community. They should make you rethink all the investment advice you've ever heard.

The report analyzes the three primary investment strategies that determine variations in portfolio performance: market timing, security selection, and asset allocation. Here's what should concern you: The two strategies that have the least impact on performance variation are market timing and security selection. Market timing and security selection activities rely on attempts to predict the future. Most stockbrokers' recommendations are based on these two strategies. Wall Street firms spend billions of dollars each year trying to outguess the competition in these two areas. On average, these two strategies do not add value. In most studies, not only do they not add value but after management fees, they significantly underperform the market.

The third strategy—asset allocation—has the largest effect on portfolio performance variation, and it is the simplest of the three to use. *Asset allocation accounts for over 90 percent of the variation in returns of a diversified portfolio.*

WHY ISN'T EVERYONE USING THESE STRATEGIES?

If Modern Portfolio Theory is so popular with institutional investors, why aren't individual investors using it? We have often wondered about this ourselves, especially since the theory is taught in every basic finance class in business schools across the country.

---

[3]Brinson, Gary P., L. Randolph Hood, and Gilbert L. Beebower, "Determinants of Portfolio Performance," *Financial Analysts Journal* (July-August 1986), pp. 39-44.

We suspect there's one main reason why the majority of the public doesn't know about Modern Portfolio Theory: Most major brokerage and financial services firms aren't in the business of educating the public. Their primary concern is maximizing their own profits. Stockbrokers are taught to drive transactions by pushing their clients' emotional hot buttons. They earn most of their money on commissions, not performance. A well-informed public could cut into brokers' profits dramatically.

Even the most senior members of the investment community have begun to question why Modern Portfolio Theory has not gained more widespread acceptance.[4] It turns out that the organizational politics of the major financial services firms has made its acceptance almost impossible.

What about the media? Aren't magazines and television shows in business to help investors make informed decisions? No. They're in business to make money for their producers and advertisers. The media thrive on volatility and uncertainty. If everyone knew how to invest scientifically and without emotion, there wouldn't be any need for media gurus. Sales of magazines and newsletters would plummet. Profits would suffer. Other people's self-interest is the main reason, then, that more individual investors aren't using these ideas.

WHAT YOU WILL LEARN FROM THIS BOOK

We have a different philosophy, a very simple one. *We believe in sharing our knowledge of investments with anyone who's interested.* Our belief that informed investors are our best clients propelled us to write this book. We believe intelligent investors will be more successful if they understand how the markets work and how easily our strategies can be implemented. So we have written this book out of enlightened self-interest: We know that we can achieve our goals if we can help enough investors achieve theirs.

Our strategies will demystify the investment management process. You will gain more control over your long-term investment returns—without the need to forecast market movements. Our methodologies will enable you to build a scientific portfolio of stocks, bonds, and cash that will allow you to be a successful investor. You'll quickly understand why these practical ideas are the standards for prudent investing all over the world. By the time you have read the first three chapters, you'll understand why more than one-third of major pension plan assets are invested according to these methods.

[4]Michaud, Richard, "The Markowitz Optimization Enigma: Is 'Optimized' Optimal?" *Financial Analysts Journal* (January-February 1989), pp. 31-42.

We begin by explaining the five fundamental needs that all successful investors must satisfy. Most people do not have a plan to address each of these needs, but ignoring them won't make them go away. We illustrate how you can safely and prudently reach all of your investment objectives while overcoming the common frustrations most investors face.

You'll learn how professionals identify and quantify investment risk. You will understand the historical risk–reward relationship between different types of investments and why some investments have consistently outperformed others. And you will discover the professional's secret for taming market volatility.

You'll learn how to use the five principles of asset class investing to balance your investment portfolio scientifically. These techniques will enable you to design portfolios with the specific levels of risk that meet your individual comfort level while maximizing your return. We explain how to counterbalance different investment classes to maximize your expected returns. This easy-to-use investment strategy has historically beaten those used by most professional managers.

We uncover the hidden costs of investing in mutual funds. We show you how, like institutional investors, you can slash your administrative and transaction costs by up to 75 percent. Any cost savings will go directly to your bottom line.

In Chapter 12, we invite you to match your risk comfort level to a scientifically designed model portfolio. These portfolios use the most cost-effective asset class building blocks available to create an efficient portfolio. In this section, you'll have an opportunity to examine your own different investment options and the most likely outcomes of each. You'll learn what you can realistically expect to earn in the individual investment portfolio you construct.

This is not a textbook; it is not written for the academic community. It is written to be a practical investment guide for the prudent individual investor. We have tried to have fun in communicating the information by taking some very technical subjects and attempting to make them understandable. We encourage you to leave all your thoughts and preconceptions about investing behind and walk with us through this process.

It is not critical that you understand everything we have written in this book. In fact, most of you will still want to work with an advisor, and that's fine. What you need to know is whether *your advisor* understands these concepts and can implement them on your behalf. In Chapter 13, we outline the questions you should ask in selecting an advisor. The ideas we present in this book will give you confidence to move forward, either with an advisor or on your own.

CHAPTER

Five Key Concepts of
Investment Success

In our work with thousands of investors of all walks of life, from individuals just getting started to the CEOs of some of the country's largest corporations, we have identified several fundamental needs facing all investors. In this chapter, we describe these five fundamental needs and show you how we successfully meet these needs for our clients using our five key concepts of investment success, and how you can use them to meet your own needs.

INVESTOR NEED 1: RISK REDUCTION

Investors are risk averse. Actually, they are loss averse—they don't like *losing* money. You may remember what Michael Douglas, playing Gordon Gekko, said in the movie *Wall Street*: "I don't like losses, sport. Nothing ruins my day more than losses." No one likes losses. Therefore, we need to better understand risk so that we can weather short-term losses while not losing sight of our long-term goals.

Few investors truly understand the concept of risk. If more people understood risk, far fewer investors would be disappointed with their results. Unfortunately, most investors do not know the risks they are taking. Many investment risks are inappropriate, resulting in huge numbers of lawsuits and arbitration hearings. Because of risk aversion and lack of knowledge about risk, billions of dollars sit in bank savings and money market accounts, yielding approximately the same as the inflation rate.

A key component of any investment plan is understanding and measuring risk. Risk is simply the uncertainty of future results. It is created by the volatility of the marketplace. Volatility is the range of up and down movements in a price of a security. Will Rogers used to say, "Don't tell me about the return *on* my money until you tell me about the return *of* my money." The less certain you are that an investment's actual return will equal its expected return, the more risk that investment carries.

Most investors recognize that they are taking some risk, but they don't know how to quantify the amount. Even Treasury bills, which are generally considered to be a risk-free investment, are subject to inflation risk. When you calculate the net return of Treasury bills after taxes and inflation, you are often assured of little or no return at all. Prudent investors want to know how to best safeguard their life savings. They do so by understanding the trade-off between risk and return. By embracing the level of risk with which you feel comfortable, you can control risk and maximize return.

The historical risk of an investment can be statistically measured using standard deviation. Standard deviation describes how far from the mean (average) the historical performance has been. Although the deviation can be either higher or lower, it's the *downside* deviation that is painful. If the distribution is normal, one standard deviation added to or subtracted from the mean encompasses about 68 percent of the occurrences, and two standard deviations cover approximately 95 percent of them. For example, Figure 2-1 shows that, from January 1926 to December

FIGURE 2-1

Standard Deviation as a Measure of Risk

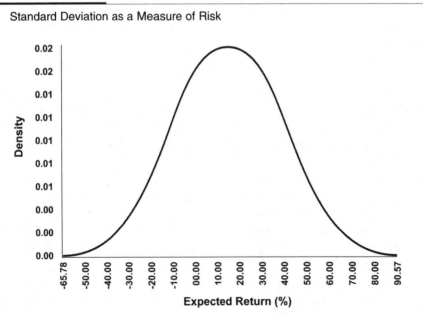

Source: Ibbotson Associates

1997, the average arithmetic annual return of the S&P 500 Index is 13.0 percent, and its standard deviation is 20.3 percent. We would expect the distribution of returns to fall between –7.3 percent and 33.3 percent approximately 68 percent of the time, given the S&P 500's historical standard deviation. Remember, the wider the range of returns, the more risk there is in the investment.

Figure 2-1 illustrates a normal bell-shaped distribution. The actual monthly distributions for the S&P 500 are not as neat. While the actual results are not a perfect normal distribution, the standard deviation measure helps to explain what the distribution is likely to be.

Risk can be classified into two broad categories: loss of principal and loss of purchasing power. The risk of losing principal comes from investing in securities whose value fluctuates due to systematic risk, unsystematic risk, or both. Systematic risk cannot be diversified away. It is the risk that is common to the market as a whole. An extra return, or risk premium, is demanded by investors to bear this kind of risk because it cannot be diversified away. Nonsystematic risk, on the other hand, can be completely eliminated with diversification. Nonsystematic risk is the specific risk associated with an individual security. Because it can be so easily eliminated with diversification, the market does not reward investors with a return premium for taking this kind of risk. We recommend, therefore, that you completely diversify your portfolio to eliminate all nonsystematic risk.

The risk of losing purchasing power is generally derived from investing in assets whose realized rates of return are too low to compensate for the erosion of principal by taxes and inflation. There is clearly a risk involved in investing too conservatively. You must accept some uncertainty in your investments if you are to generate positive returns after accounting for inflation and taxes.

Each investor has a unique risk tolerance level. Your risk tolerance can be characterized by the amount of short-term loss you are willing to accept in order to achieve your long-term goals. You should not take more risk than you are comfortable with; doing so is the surest road to financial failure. If there is a market downturn and you are taking too much risk, you might panic and sell your positions. However, if you design your portfolio with your risk tolerance in mind, you will be able to ride out a downturn and achieve investment success. In Chapter 9, we show you how to calculate your own risk tolerance.

INVESTOR NEED 2: RETURN ENHANCEMENT

If you are like most investors, you want the highest return possible. Most people, when they make an investment decision, try to find the investment that will give them the highest return. Unfortunately, they don't consider risk or how the investment fits with the other assets in their portfolios. Basically, most of us want candy (high returns) when what we really need is a balanced meal (a well-diversified portfolio).

Furthermore, most investors believe there is a guru out there who can point out the investments with high returns and little or, better yet, no risk. "If only I search a little harder," they say to themselves, "I can find the right oracle." After all, one might say, "If I can identify Michael Jordan and Tiger Woods in the sports world, why can't I do the same in the investment world?" The media reinforce this mentality by making folk heroes out of successful investment managers like George Soros, Warren Buffet, and Peter Lynch. All too often, investors make investment decisions based on the predictions and recommendations of "experts." This usually results in disappointment, regret, and cynicism.

Success does not come from finding a guru who promises wealth without risk, but in understanding *how markets work*. Investors should become familiar with the underlying concepts of diversification, rather than focusing on the last few years of a mutual fund's performance. The challenge every investor faces in the quest for return enhancement is to resist getting caught up in the numerous financial magazines and investment newsletter publications that play to our emotions, often with contradictory advice. Remember, they are in business to sell magazines, not to make money for you.

Unfortunately, most investors are noise investors. They believe that by reading the *Wall Street Journal* each morning they become "insiders" with enough knowledge to beat the market. Noise investors think they are trading on information that gives them an advantage, but most of them lose money. Noise investors do, however, have one redeeming quality: They provide increased liquidity for information investors. Information investors understand how financial markets work, and they use this knowledge to make money consistently and prudently.[1] In Chapter 3, we show you how to move away from the noise and become an information investor.

Expected return is the forecasted arithmetic average return based on long-term historical data and future probability assumptions. Expected returns are theoretical returns; they are not guarantees of future performance. However, calculating expected rates of return along with estimates of correlation (the degree to which two assets move together) provides you with a benchmark to determine whether or not that investment is appropriate for your portfolio. It also provides a framework for measuring results. This allows you to stay on track and evaluate how you're doing.

[1]Black, Fischer, "Noise," *Journal of Finance* (July 1986), pp. 529-543. The concept of noise and information investors was developed from this article.

INVESTOR NEED 3: MEETING A FUTURE FINANCIAL OBJECTIVE

Everyone has financial goals they want to achieve. Maybe you want to have enough money to send your children or grandchildren to college, to enjoy financial independence, or to provide for a comfortable retirement. Your goals may change through the years, but what determines investment success will not. Your investment success will be determined by three factors:

1. the amount of money you invest,
2. the rate of return you realize, and
3. the length of time your money has to grow.

The primary goal of most investors is a secure retirement. They want to be able to live comfortably without outliving their money. Can you think of anything more frightening than to be 85 years old, in perfect health, but without any money?

In the study represented in Figure 2-2, investors indicated that securing their retirement was their number one goal, with educating their children a close second. What are your goals? Make a list of your goals and prioritize them; you will use them in the investment policy statement we show you how to write in Chapter 10.

FIGURE 2-2

Areas of Concern

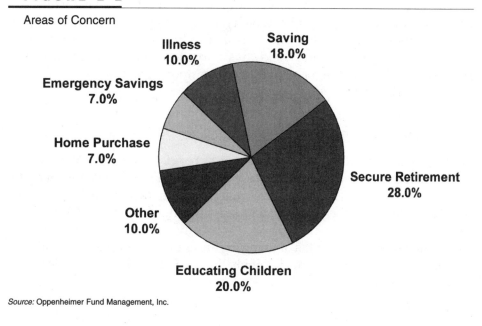

Source: Oppenheimer Fund Management, Inc.

INVESTOR NEED 4: PROVIDING A DEPENDABLE INCOME STREAM

To reach financial independence, you will have to develop a dependable income stream to meet your living expenses. But remember, the income stream you need today will not be the income stream you need tomorrow. For example, if you were planning your retirement in 1974, you might have budgeted your income needs based on houses that cost $35,000, cars that cost less than $5,000, and gas at under 30 cents a gallon. What may have been a very comfortable income in 1974 would be difficult to live on today. For example, due to inflation, it takes $3.51 today to equal the purchasing power of $1.00 in 1974.[2] In other words, if you retired with an annual income of $30,000 in 1974, today you would need an income of about $105,000 to have the same purchasing power! Think how this would have affected your family's lifestyle. Your income must grow over time to allow for the increasing cost of living.

Most investors know they need to invest for a dependable income stream, but they don't know how to secure it and they often make costly mistakes. The most common mistake we see is holding a portfolio of securities that generates a desired level of income solely from dividends and interest. The drawback to this approach is that it forces you to choose investments based on current yields. A portfolio put together this way lacks diversification; it has too many high-yielding securities such as utilities, preferred stocks, long-term bonds, and high-yield bonds. These securities do not combine to make a good portfolio because they share interest rate sensitivity as a common risk factor. We suggest that you take a *total return approach* in building your portfolio, which means you get the income you need not only from dividends and interest, but also from the liquidation of capital gains. Instead of chasing yield, this approach allows you to focus on building a well-diversified portfolio that is properly balanced and sensitive to different risk factors.

INVESTOR NEED 5: MAINTAINING LIQUIDITY

Your portfolio should help you prepare for a financial emergency. Without access to immediate cash you cannot take fast action. Liquidity is the ability to turn your investments into cash quickly at current market value. Investments that lack liquidity either prevent you from getting your money quickly or force you to sell at discounted prices. An effective rule of thumb is that you should have about six months of living expenses in cash equivalents, with the remainder of your investments in highly liquid, easily valued securities.

[2]Calculated using the Consumer Price Index from January 1974 through November 1997.

HOW MUCH INCOME IS SAFE?

Someday, you may want to take income from your investment nest egg. For most investors this occurs at retirement, but it could occur earlier if you need supplemental income before you stop working. We have found a lot of confusion and misinformation about how much income one can safely withdraw from a portfolio without risking significant depletion of principal over time.

For many years, endowments and foundations such as colleges, universities, churches, and nonprofits have researched the subject of sustainable withdrawal rates from long-term investment portfolios. Endowment and foundation funds are managed to sustain the research, capital spending, and operations of their underlying institutions. Their portfolios must exist in perpetuity, as well as pay out sufficient income each year. In the end, they must not spend more than the real return on their investments. This is the only way they can be assured that their assets will last forever.

Although individual investors are different from endowments and foundations, those of you who are saving for retirement income have similar goals. In fact, we encourage you to think of your retirement portfolio as a *mini endowment fund*. Although your endowment fund does not need to last forever, it does need to last as long as you and your spouse are alive. Like endowment funds, most investors also want to get as much income as they can, without reducing principal in real terms.

Endowments and foundations have developed three guiding principles for managing their investments:

1. **Assets should be invested in fixed income and equity securities.** The typical endowment fund is invested 60 percent in equities and 40 percent in fixed income securities.

2. **Assets must be effectively diversified.** Endowments diversify their equity investments into asset classes that are relatively uncorrelated in order to reduce risk. They follow multi-asset, total return investment policies.

3. **A conservative spending rate of 5 percent of invested assets per year is recommended.** The typical endowment spending policy is 5 percent.[3]

We suggest that you follow these principles when investing for retirement income. In Table 2-1 we show the annual income you can expect from different portfolio values.

[3]The required withdrawal rate for most endowments is 5 percent, as mandated by the Tax Reform Act of 1969.

TABLE 2-1

Portfolio Value	Annual Income 5% Withdrawal Rate
$250,000	$12,500
$500,000	$25,000
$750,000	$37,500
$1,000,000	$50,000
$1,500,000	$75,000
$2,000,000	$100,000
$5,000,000	$250,000
$10,000,000	$500,000

These withdrawals may seem small, but you should be conservative so that your income can grow over time to cover rising prices. Remember to factor into your retirement income projections the expected after-tax growth of your portfolio, as well as the expected erosion of purchasing power due to inflation.

START WITH A CLEAN SHEET OF PAPER

Once you have reviewed your financial needs, you are in a position to design an investment program to meet them. A popular concept that has recently been getting a lot of attention in business management circles is process management, often referred to as reengineering. The concept is nothing new. It amounts to knowing where you are, where you want to go, and how you are going to get there without becoming distracted along the way.

You can use many reengineering techniques to get started in building your investment program. We recommend that you begin with a clean sheet of paper. For the moment, set aside your own biases and what you may have read in popular investment magazines. Remember the printed media's not-so-hidden agenda: They want to sell magazines and advertising space. They accomplish this by playing to your fears and emotions.

Instead of getting investment advice from journalists, let's go to the informed sources—the best and brightest scholars of academic finance. We are very fortunate that the academic community has accumulated a tremendous body of knowledge, taking a scientific view of investment markets and how they work. You need to know what they've learned if you want to be successful.

THE MEDIA AND MISINFORMATION

For several years the media have been telling us that U.S. stock prices have been going up because of large inflows of new money into stock mutual funds. The market is relying on the new money, they say, and if the money flow slows, the market will suffer. This idea sounds like it makes sense, but it is factually misleading and theoretically wrong.

The reality is that according to Federal Reserve data, on average, individual investors have been net sellers of stocks, not buyers, over most of the last 30 years. In addition, the percentage of individual investors' financial assets held in stocks has changed very little since the late 1960s. What's happened is that the popularity of defined contribution plans, such as 401(k)s, has caused significant new money to flow into stock mutual funds in recent years, giving the appearance that new money is going into the stock market. There is, however, a missing element to the story. Individuals also hold stocks directly, and have been significant net sellers of directly held issues.

For the moment, let's ignore the net selling of directly held issues by individuals and focus on the purchases of equities by mutual funds. Table 2-2 shows the net purchases of equities by mutual funds from 1982 to 1996, including the corresponding annual returns of the S&P 500 index. If cash flow into mutual funds is really driving the stock market, we should see a direct correlation between mutual fund stock purchases and overall market performance. The data show that there is no such relationship—the correlation is zero. Stock purchases (or sales) by mutual funds are independent of, and have no direct effect on, market performance.

TABLE 2-2

Year	Net Purchases of Equities by Mutual Funds ($bil)	S&P 500 Return (%)
1982	2.8	21.4
1983	13.1	22.5
1984	5.4	6.3
1985	9.9	32.2
1986	23.1	18.5
1987	30.2	5.2
1988	-13.2	16.8
1989	0.9	31.5
1990	14.5	-3.2
1991	50.3	30.5
1992	59.8	7.7
1993	117.1	1.0
1994	10.6	1.3
1995	81.2	37.4
1996	190.5	23.1
Correlation Between Purchases and Returns		**-0.03**

Source: Federal Reserve Board

This should not be surprising. There shouldn't be a direct relationship between mutual fund stock purchases and stock prices. Why? Because the money that goes into stock mutual funds is used to buy stock from someone who already owns it. The amount of stock purchased is exactly equal to the amount sold. Therefore, in the aggregate, any net purchases of stock by mutual funds must be exactly offset by net sales of stock from other sources. So stock prices are not dependent upon stock mutual fund purchases or cash flows into mutual funds.

According to the classic dividend discount model, the price of a stock is equal to the discounted present value of expected future dividends. The two important variables are the discount rate k and the expected growth rate of dividends g. All else equal, if k rises (falls), then the stock price will fall (rise), and if g increases (decreases), then the stock price will rise (fall). Under this model, valuation has nothing to do with new money coming into the market.

THE FIVE KEY CONCEPTS OF INVESTMENT SUCCESS

Investing can at times seem overwhelming, but it can be broken down into five simple, key concepts. In investing just as in all of life, it's the simpler things that consistently work.

Concept 1: Utilize diversification effectively to reduce risk.

Most of us understand the basic concept of diversification: Don't put all your eggs in one basket. However, no matter how sophisticated we are, it's easy to get caught in a trap. For example, many investors have a large part of their investment capital in their employer's stock, even though they understand that they are probably taking too much risk. They justify holding the position because of the large capital gains tax they would have to pay if they sold it; or they imagine that the stock is just about to take off. Often, they are so close to the company that they get emotionally tied to the stock and develop a false sense of comfort.

We work in California's Silicon Valley. A very high percentage of our clients have watched their companies go public and have become millionaires. Unfortunately, too many do not understand the risk they are taking by maintaining their positions rather than diversifying. We believe that what *made* these executives rich may not *keep* them rich—as they say, risk happens. They would still be able to reach their families' financial goals even after paying the capital gains tax, if only they would diversify. Unfortunately, some learn the error of their ways only after their stock has plummeted and they are no longer on track to achieve their financial goals.

Other investors believe they have effectively diversified because they hold a dozen different stocks. They don't realize it, but they are in for an emotional roller-coaster ride if these stocks share similar risk factors—if the stocks are part of the same industry group or asset class. For example, we often talk with investors who feel they are diversified because they own a variety of different high-technology companies. However, the reality is that most high-tech firms share similar risk factors and tend to move together. These investors are not nearly as diversified as they think they are. What about your portfolio? Are your investments concentrated in one industry or asset class? If so, you should diversify.

To help you understand the emotions of investing, think of what happens when you get a hot tip on a stock. If you are like most investors, you don't buy the stock right away. You follow it for a while to see how it does. Let's say it starts trending upward. You still don't buy it, but you begin to hope it will keep going up. If it continues its upward trend, you start to feel greed as you become convinced it's for real. So you call your broker and buy the stock. Of course, soon after you buy it, the stock starts to go down and you feel fear and regret—you are afraid you've made a terrible mistake. It continues to go down until you finally panic, and sell.

This is the emotional curve of investing (see Figure 2-3). It is a powerful force that causes you to do exactly the opposite of what you should. That is, your emotions lead you to buy high and sell low. If you do that often enough, you can cause serious damage to your retirement fund.

The overall risk of a portfolio is not the average risk of each of the investments; the overall risk is actually *less* than the average risk if your investments do not move together. In fact, you can have a low-risk portfolio that is actually made up of high-risk assets, as long as the assets in the portfolio don't move in lockstep with each other. When investments are com-

FIGURE 2-3

The Emotional Curve of Investing

bined in this way, you achieve effective diversification. Dissimilar price movement diversification protects you from having all your investments go down at the same time.

This is a profound academic investment discovery that represents a breakthrough in investment methodology. It has dramatically changed the way many investors manage money. We now recognize the importance of analyzing the relationship between assets in a portfolio, rather than evaluating each of them in isolation. You should too.

Concept 2: Dissimilar price movement diversification enhances return.

If you have two investment portfolios with the same average or arithmetic return, the portfolio with *less* volatility will have a *greater* compound or geometric rate of return. For example, let's assume that you are considering two mutual funds. Each of them has an average annual expected return of 10 percent. How would you determine which fund is better? You would probably expect them to have the same ending wealth value. However, this is only true if they have the same degree of volatility. If one fund is more volatile than the other, their compound return and ending values will be different. It is a mathematical fact that the one with less volatility will have a greater compound return.

In Figure 2-4, portfolio A is much less volatile than portfolio B and, consequently, has a greater compound rate of return and a higher ending value.

FIGURE 2-4

Two Portfolios with the Same Average Rate of Return

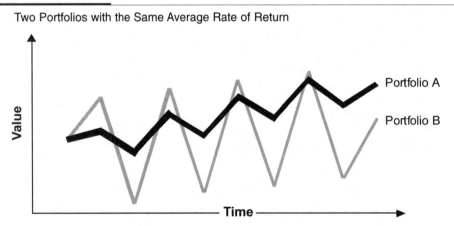

FIGURE 2-5

Investment Philosophies

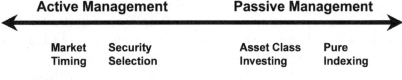

Use this key concept of investment success to combine investments within a portfolio that don't move together, thus reducing the volatility of the portfolio. This strategy will enhance your compound returns and give you a greater ending wealth.

Concept 3: Employ asset class investing.

Most investors who understand the first two concepts use conventional mutual funds to implement them. That's like trying to fix a sink with a screwdriver when you really need a pipe wrench. In other words, use the right tools. Asset class mutual funds are the right tools.

In Figure 2-5, we summarize four different investment philosophies available to investors. About 97 percent of retail mutual funds use active management strategies. Although there are many active management techniques, they basically involve market timing, security selection, or a combination of both. Market timing is the attempt to be in the market when it goes up and be out of the market when it goes down. Security selection involves trying to identify securities that are undervalued and will deliver market-beating returns. The common link between these strategies is that they involve subjective forecasting, and the likelihood of human error that accompanies it. The pickers and timers of active management don't believe markets work. They think prices adjust slowly enough that they can systematically uncover incorrectly priced securities and add value beyond the added management and trading costs. We cannot find any empirical or theoretical justification for active management.

Passive management, on the other hand, rests on the sound theoretical framework that free and competitive markets work, and that assets are priced fairly and reflect all known information. Passive investing involves capturing the risk and return dimensions of an entire asset class by buying and holding a large basket of securities. An asset class is a group of investment securities whose risk factors and expected returns are similar.

There are two methods of passive investing: pure indexing and asset class investing. Pure indexing is an attempt to deliver the returns of a predetermined, usually well-known index of stocks or bonds. An S&P 500 Index fund is by far the most common index fund for both institutional and individual investors. It tracks the performance of the Standard & Poor's 500 Index, a capitalization-weighted index of 500 large U.S. stocks. We estimate that over 95 percent of all retail investors' money that is indexed is invested in S&P 500 Index funds.

Asset class investing is similar to pure indexing in that it delivers the returns of an asset class without subjective forecasting. However, it differs from pure indexing in its implementation. *Asset class funds are not forced to precisely track an arbitrary paper index of securities.* Instead, they retain the flexibility to make trading and portfolio construction decisions that add value. We believe asset class funds combine the best of active and passive strategies. They offer the consistency, low costs, and low turnover of passive management, along with the flexibility to make intelligent trading and portfolio construction decisions that add value.

Concept 4: Global diversification reduces risk.

In 1996, world equity markets were more than 20 times larger than they were in 1970. While the U.S. market is still the largest equity market, its relative size has decreased significantly compared with the world equity market as a whole. For example, in 1970 the international equity market represented only 32 percent of total world equities. By 1996, non-U.S. markets made up 57 percent of total world equities.[3] In building your portfolio, you should consider the diversification opportunities available in the international markets.

In Figure 2-6, we compare the relative performance of U.S. stocks and foreign stocks from January 1970 to December 1997.

We do this by subtracting the rolling 12-month return of the S&P 500 Index from Morgan Stanley's Europe-Australia-Far East (EAFE) Index. The EAFE Index is comprised of approximately 1,000 large company stocks spread across the world, excluding the United States, while the S&P 500 capture the returns of 500 large U.S. stocks. When the shaded area is above zero, the U.S. equity market outperforms the foreign markets. When the shaded area is below zero, the foreign markets outperform the U.S. equity market.

[3]Morgan Stanley Capital International Perspective, Geneva, Switzerland.

FIGURE 2-6

Performance of U.S. and Foreign Markets

January 1969-December 1997

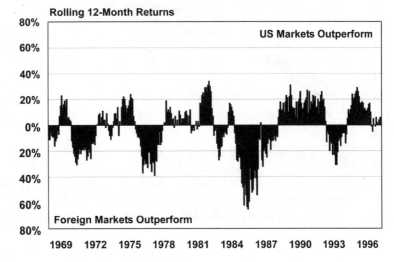

Source: Ibbotson Associates and Morgan Stanley Capital International

This is a clear example of dissimilar price movement and the value of diversification. We see long periods when the U.S. equity market either outperforms or underperforms foreign markets. You can reduce risk by allocating a portion of your portfolio to foreign stocks. Foreign equity exposure can both lower risk and increase the expected return of your portfolio. With global diversification, you protect yourself from downturns in any one country's market and you receive returns equal to the global cost of capital.

Concept 5: Design portfolios that are efficient.

How do we decide which investments to own and in what combination? For more than 25 years major institutions have been using a money management concept known as Modern Portfolio Theory to help them answer this question. Modern Portfolio Theory was developed at the University of Chicago by Harry Markowitz and Merton Miller and later expanded by Stanford professor William Sharpe. Markowitz, Miller, and Sharpe won the Nobel Prize in Economics in 1990 for their contributions to Modern Portfolio Theory. The five-step process of developing a strategic portfolio

FIGURE 2-7

The Range of Efficient Portfolios

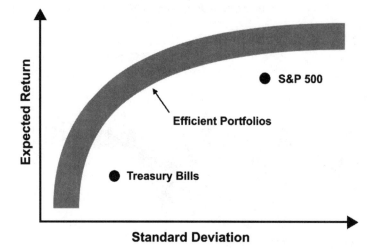

using Modern Portfolio Theory is mathematical in nature and can, at times, appear daunting. Yet, as you examine the process, you'll see the common-sense approach they have taken.

Markowitz states that for every level of risk there is some optimal combination of investments that will give you the highest rate of return. The range of portfolios exhibiting this optimal risk–reward trade-off forms the efficient frontier, shown in Figure 2-7. The efficient frontier is determined by calculating the expected rate of return, standard deviation, and correlation coefficient for each asset class and using this information to find the range of portfolios with the highest expected return for any given level of risk. By plotting each portfolio representing a given level of risk and expected return, we are able to find a series of efficient portfolios.

Most investors' portfolios fall significantly below the efficient frontier. Even a portfolio such as the S&P 500, which is often used as a proxy for the U.S. market, falls below the line. Figure 2-7 shows the efficient frontier relative to the S&P 500. Prudent investors will restrict their choice of portfolios to those that appear in the range of efficient portfolios at their chosen level of risk. In Chapter 8, you will learn how these optimal portfolios are built.

Unfortunately, the concepts of Modern Portfolio Theory are not widely understood and are often misapplied. They represent a new investment paradigm—a profound body of knowledge that has revolution-ized Wall Street, but not Main Street. The truth is that many investors are making the most important financial decisions of their lives based on mis-conceptions about how markets work. After reading this book, you will be well informed and able to avoid those misconceptions.

3 CHAPTER

From Noise to Information

This chapter will help you break through the false beliefs that many noise investors share and start on the road to becoming a successful information investor.

Here is the problem: Noise is not fact, even when it represents the conventional wisdom of the time. Unfortunately, conventional wisdom is extremely difficult to change. Consider the ideas of Claudius Ptolemy who, around 100 A.D., mistakenly placed the earth at the center of the universe. Based on this false belief, he developed a comprehensive system for tracing the motion of the planets and calculated the orbits of each of them. Soon he had compiled a 13-volume work that was the accepted authoritative source throughout Europe for over 1,200 years.

Fortunately, Nicholas Copernicus questioned Ptolemy's work and formulated his own theory—one that placed the sun at the center of our universe and the earth as a planet rotating around it. His findings showed Ptolemy's ideas to be erroneous.

Just as Claudius Ptolemy's work was ultimately questioned and later found to be false, we have learned that many commonly held investment principles are based on false assumptions. This is good news. It means there is an easier and more sensible road to investment success.

Galileo used his new invention, the telescope, to show Pope Paul V that Copernicus' theory was accurate—that the earth, in fact, rotates around the sun. For challenging conventional wisdom, church officials sentenced him to an indefinite prison term.

Thousands of people have built careers and businesses around currently accepted investment principles. But the truth is, there is no scientific basis for many of the most highly touted beliefs, including the idea that value is added through primary techniques of active management—stock selection and market timing. These beliefs are for the most part a collection of false assumptions. When you finally sift the truth from these faulty paradigms, it is no wonder most people have come to distrust the investment community.

Constant change is one thing in life that is always certain. You cannot afford to ignore the facts, no matter how compelling the outdated, unsubstantiated beliefs. You must let go of old thoughts and embrace new ideas. We hope that after reading this book you will have the courage to be different. No one who challenged conventional investment wisdom has ever been sentenced to prison.

USING THE INVESTMENT METHODOLOGY DECISION MATRIX

Wall Street likes investment noise because of the effect it has on investor behavior. Investment noise causes uncertainty, confusion, and fear. In short, it encourages investors to move money—and lots of it. On the New York Stock Exchange, for example, the average daily trading volume is over 500 million shares, which represents $20 billion of market value. This activity is usually unproductive and costly, but most investors fall into the trap of believing it adds value.

We share the matrix in Figure 3-1 to illustrate a point that we first learned from Roger Gibson, author of *Asset Allocation*. This matrix classifies

FIGURE 3·1

Investment Decision Matrix

		Market Timing	
		Yes	No
Security Selection	Yes	**Noise Quadrant** **1** Most Individual Investors Financial Journalists	**Conventional Wisdom Quadrant** **2** Financial Planners Stock Brokers Most Mutual Funds
	No	**Tactical Allocation Quadrant** **3** Pure Market Timers Asset Allocation Funds	**Information Quadrant** **4** Academics 40% of Institutional Investors

investors according to what they believe is effective in adding value. Identify the quadrant into which you currently fit. Our goal in this chapter is to move you to the quadrant that insures the highest probability of success.

Quadrant one is the noise quadrant. It is composed of investors who believe in both market timing and security selection. They think they or their favorite guru can consistently uncover mispriced securities that will deliver market-beating returns. In addition, they believe it is possible to identify the mispricing of an entire market, and predict when it will turn up or down. The reality is that the vast majority of these methods fail to even match the market, let alone beat it. Unfortunately, most of the public is in this quadrant and much of the media plays to this thinking.

Quadrant two is the conventional wisdom quadrant. It includes most of the financial services industry. Most investment professionals have the experience to know that they can't predict broad market swings with any degree of accuracy. They know that making incorrect predictions usually means losing clients. However, they believe their thousands of market analysts and portfolio managers with MBAs and high-tech information systems can find undervalued securities and add value for their clients. Of course, it's the American Dream to believe that, if you're bright enough and work hard enough, you will be successful in a competitive environment. Unfortunately, as un-American as it seems, in an efficient capital market this methodology adds no value on average.

Quadrant three is the tactical allocation quadrant. Investors in this quadrant somehow believe that, even though individual securities are priced efficiently, they and only they can see broad mispricing in entire markets sectors. They think they can add value by buying when a market is undervalued, waiting until the rest of investors finally recognize their mistake, and selling when the market is fairly valued once again. We believe it is inconsistent to think that individual securities are priced fairly, but that overall markets, which are aggregates of the fairly priced individual securities, are not. No prudent investors are found in this quadrant.

Quadrant four is the information quadrant. This is where most of the academic community resides, as well as 40 percent of all institutional investors. Investors in this quadrant dispassionately research what works and then follow a rational course of action based on empirical evidence. Academic studies indicate that the average returns of the first three quadrants are negative rather than positive. *Quadrant 4 is where you should be*, and where you will find all prudent investors.

Unfortunately, it is hard to be dispassionate and logical about our money. Most people want to believe in gurus and want to think that market timing, stock selection, and active management add value. But it is important for you to recognize that you won't be successful if you are caught up in the noise.

Our clients tell us that moving from noise to information is one of the most liberating experiences of their lives. As information investors, they recognize the noise for what it is and no longer pay attention to noise-based investment advice.

Unfortunately, we cannot accept any new body of knowledge until the chains of our old beliefs are broken. So let's start breaking the chains of false investment beliefs. We will dramatically change the way you think about investing and how financial markets work, so that you can make smart decisions about your money.

THE BEGINNING OF AN INVESTMENT PARADIGM SHIFT

The academic community started questioning the financial markets in the early 1900s. The first questions arose when a French mathematician named Louis Bachelier set out to study statistics.[1] While working toward his Ph.D. in mathematics at the University of Paris, Bachelier decided to study the behavior of the future markets on French government bonds, which traded on the Bourse. He wanted to explore the mathematical properties of these futures, so he examined a series of market price changes. He attempted to use the numbers statistically to see if there was a way to determine market movements using past trends. Bachelier discovered what later would become one of the core concepts of modern finance theory: *There is no useful information contained in historical price movements of securities.* In other words, there are no patterns and there is no ability to predict future prices based on the past. His study was lost and was never really looked at again until after World War II. Eventually, though, his work set the stage for the next investigation by academics.

In the 1950s, when universities and certain research institutions got their hands on computers, researchers naturally wanted to use the new tools to analyze data. Some of the first computer applications were analyses of returns on stock market indices and individual stocks and bonds. The academic community began analyzing these data with no particular theory or hypothesis in mind, only the desire to learn from whatever they might discover. It is no coincidence that a number of academics working in different places—Holbrook Working and Harry Roberts[2] at the Univer-

---

[1]Bachelier, Louis, *Theory of Speculation*, trans. A. James Boness (Paris: Gauthier Villars, 1900). Reprinted in Cootner (ed.), *The Random Character of Stock Market Prices*, Cambridge, MA, M.I.T. Press, 1964.

[2]Roberts, Harry V., "Stock Market Patterns and Financial Analysis: Methodological Suggestions," *Journal of Finance* (March 1959), pp. 1–10.

sity of Chicago, Neil Osborne[3] at IBM Research, and others—all discovered the same things.

What they found was that time series of price changes are serially uncorrelated. This means there is no predictability from one price to the next. Just as Bachelier had discovered 50 years earlier, the price series for daily, weekly, monthly, and annual outcomes all appeared to be random. Prior price data uncovers no knowledge of what the following price might be. A computer generating a series of random and unrelated numbers would have given the same result. The academic community was beginning to understand *why market forecasting is impossible.*

In one study, Maurice Kendall concluded that stock prices follow a "random walk" and are thus unpredictable as long as investors share all relevant information on the stock in question.[4] One could compare a random walk to a coin flipping contest. It is widely believed that the law of averages ensures that in a long coin-tossing game each player will be on the winning side about half the time, with the lead passing frequently from one player to the other. When a coin is flipped 10,000 times, one would think that the lead would change hands every second or third flip, but statistically it happens only about every 100 flips. Contrary to popular belief, the laws governing a prolonged series of coin flips show patterns and averages far removed from those you might expect.

If a simple coin-tossing game leads to paradoxical results that contradict our intuition, then our intuition cannot possibly serve as a reliable guide in the more complicated securities market. In Figure 3-2, we used a random number generator to simulate 10,000 coin-tosses. The length of the interludes between successive passes across the axis may surprise you.

We know that a coin toss is a random act with random results, and that future directions cannot be predicted based on past information. Interestingly, the coin-toss analysis bears a surprising resemblance to price changes in the securities markets. With coin flipping, the expected rate of return is zero (for you to win, the other person must lose). In the financial markets, however, this is not the case. The average annual compound rate of return for the last 72 years in the S&P 500 has been 11.0 percent.[5] If we sloped the charts displayed in Figure 3-2 with a rate of return of 10 percent, they would look very much like a chart of the performance of the stock market as a whole.

[3]Osborne, N.F.M., "Brownian Motion in the Stock Market," *Operational Research* (March-April 1959), pp.145–173.

[4]Kendall, Maurice G., "The Analysis of Time Series, Part I: Prices," *Journal of the Royal Statistical Society,* 96 (1953), pp. 11–25.

[5]Ibbotson, Roger G. and Rex A. Sinquefield, "Stocks, Bonds, Bills, and Inflation: Year-by-Year Historical Returns (1926–1974)," *Journal of Business* (January 1976), pp.11–43.

FIGURE 3-2

Results of 10,000 Coin Tosses

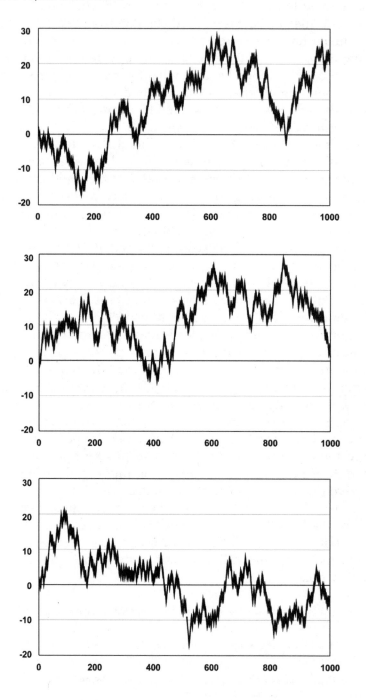

If you flip a coin, you know that about half the time it is going to come up heads and about half the time it is going to come up tails. Even if you consistently flipped heads 20 times in a row, that doesn't tell you anything about the next flip. You are just as likely to flip heads again as you are to flip tails. The effect of not being able to predict future price movements by past information is known as a random walk. In the financial markets, a random walk suggests that *you cannot determine what is going to happen next by analyzing historical price movements.*

Ever since Kendall's study was published, controversy has surrounded the random walk hypothesis. A strict interpretation of Kendall's results would imply that no technique of stock portfolio selection could consistently outperform a simple buy-and-hold strategy, using a broadly diversified group of securities. In other words, the most popular market indices that represent broad segments of the marketplace should consistently outperform the majority of professional money managers. According to former Princeton University professor Burton Malkiel, "A blindfolded chimpanzee throwing darts at the stock pages of the *Wall Street Journal* could select a portfolio that performs as well as one carefully chosen by the experts."[6]

The truth is that no one can predict the future, although many will try to convince you that they can. In short, past information doesn't tell you anything about the future. The Securities and Exchange Commission seems to believe this since they require all public offerings and advertising to state that past performance is no indicator of future performance. You should heed this warning.

Harry Roberts, a professor emeritus of statistics at the University of Chicago's Business School, completed another seminal study in 1959.[7] Rather than doing the same type of esoteric statistical analysis that other academics were doing, he reversed the whole process. He had a computer generate a series of 50 random numbers in a normal distribution with a mean of .5 percent and a standard deviation of 2 percent. The resulting mean value of plus or minus 2 percent corresponds roughly to the typical weekly price change of the average stock. Obviously there are no predictable trends in these numbers; by their very construction, this series of numbers is random. By arbitrarily starting off with a price of $40, Roberts used the random patterns to develop a graph that looked like stock price movements.

[6]Malkiel, Burton G., *A Random Walk Down Wall Street* (New York: Norton & Company, Inc., 1973).

[7]Roberts, Harry V., "Stock Market Patterns and Financial Analysis: Methodological Suggestions," *Journal of Finance* (March 1959), pp. 1–10.

Roberts placed a stock name on each chart and took them to La Salle Street in Chicago, which at that time was the hotbed of technical analysis in the universe. Technical analysis attempts to predict future trends of securities by examining the charts created by plotting past prices. Roberts took six or seven of his charts to each of the leading technicians of the day. He introduced himself and asked for advice about how to play the stock market based on this random data. Naturally, every one of the technicians had a very strong opinion about what he ought to do with each of the securities.

The patterns that the chartists observed and speculated about were randomly generated by a computer. There were, by construction, *no* actual patterns and *no* information. The patterns were in the minds of the analysts, not in the data. Even today, technical experts point out what the market is going to do next based on the shape and pattern of a chart. Unfortunately, they do not understand how markets work. They are caught up in the noise.

Conventional wisdom followed by money managers in the 1950s was to focus on picking winners; the rule of the day was to concentrate holdings so as to maximize return without diversifying. One of the leading stockbrokers on Wall Street at the time, Gerald Loeb, stated, "Once you obtain confidence, diversification is undesirable... diversification [is] an admission of not knowing what to do and an effort to strike an average."

The conventional wisdom in the 1960s was that large and persistent differences between market prices and true values existed in the stock market. Therefore, skilled investment managers could identify and exploit these differences. It was recognized that the markets were more efficient than in the 1950s, but if you worked hard enough, many thought, you could still exploit the mispricings.

Throughout the 1960s and early 1970s, the focus of most academic work involved estimating the degree of market efficiency to see if mispricing really existed. In 1965 Professor Eugene Fama of the University of Chicago wrote an authoritative thesis, coining the phrase "efficient markets" and explaining that markets appear to fully absorb new information so that prices reflect all known information.[8] In his empirical tests he found:

1. Past prices are of no value in predicting future prices.
2. Publicly available information cannot be used to earn excess returns consistently.
3. Mutual fund managers as a group cannot beat the market.

---

[8]Fama, Eugene F., "The Behavior of Stock Prices," *Journal of Business* (January 1965), pp. 34–105.

Since 1965 there have been many more tests of market efficiency that have confirmed Fama's conclusions.

TESTS OF MARKET EFFICIENCY

We believe the most telling tests of market efficiency are those that examine the performance of mutual funds, because mutual fund results are the most widely distributed and accurately reported of all professional money management efforts. Michael Jensen presented the first comprehensive study of this sort by reviewing the performance of mutual fund portfolios from 1945 to 1964.[9] The managers of mutual funds are among the best and the brightest in the investment community. If anyone can exploit inefficiencies in the market, these experts should be able to do it. What Jensen found, however, is that they cannot. His study showed that the majority of managers significantly underperform the market; in fact, only 26 out of 115 mutual funds were able to beat the market. If professional investors cannot beat the market, who can?

In 1964, an article published in *American Economic Review* by Richard Ipolitto shocked the academic community.[10] In his report, Ipolitto claimed that managers as a group could beat markets, even after expenses, and that markets were inefficient. This was an amazing result, giving Ipolitto plenty of press coverage. Could it be that the previous academic studies were wrong—that managers actually can beat the market?

Edwin Elton and several associates recently completed a review of Ipolitto's work.[11] They studied the same set of funds, but quickly found they could not duplicate his results. Why not? It turned out that Ipolitto's conclusions were largely due to data entry errors. Interestingly, all of his mistakes favored the mutual fund managers. The excess performance was wiped out after Elton's team corrected for these errors. Consistent with the results of other studies, Elton's group found that mutual fund managers on average underperform markets by significantly more than their fees.

Things have not changed since these studies were done. For example, only 14 of the 181 domestic equity funds that had been in existence for the 15 years ending December 31, 1997 had beaten the S&P 500 over that time

[9]Jensen, Michael C., "The Performance of Mutual Funds in the Period 1945-1964," *Financial Analysts Journal* (November 1989), pp. 587–616.

[10]Ipolitto, Richard, A. *American Economic Review* (1964).

[11]Elton, Edwin J., Martin J. Gruber, Sanjiv Das, and Matthew Hlavka, "Efficiency with Costly Information: A Reinterpretation of Evidence from Managed Portfolios," *Review of Financial Studies* (1993).

period.[12] That's a rather poor 7.7 percent success rate; and that figure does not include funds that were terminated due to poor performance—a problem we discuss later—which artificially increases the returns of the group. Perhaps a better benchmark is the Wilshire 5000 Index. It is a broader measure of the market because it includes mid- and small-cap stocks in addition to large-cap stocks. Still, only 27 of the funds, or 14.9 percent, have beaten this index over the same 15 years. No matter how you look at it, the performance of mutual funds, as a group, compares poorly to market benchmarks.

Why can't mutual funds beat the market? Simple math answers the question. Professional investors are the dominant competitors in the investment markets. In fact, they are so dominant that they basically are the market. Therefore, they are competing primarily against each other and, by definition, they cannot outperform themselves. So it's a mathematical certainty that the average mutual fund *must* underperform the market by the amount of its costs, which include operating expenses, sales loads, and trading costs. This is no surprise; it is exactly what we would expect to occur in an efficiently functioning capital market.

CAN YOU FIND THE WINNERS?

Obviously, some mutual funds do beat the market. A few have even done so over long periods. If you could identify those funds before the fact, you could beat the market. Is there any reliable way to do so?

The belief that past performance is a good predictor of future results (and is useful in picking tomorrow's winning funds) is so pervasive that

[12]Morningstar Principia Program, December 31, 1997.

TABLE 3-1

Mutual Fund Performance Persistency 1955–1964

Number of Consecutive Years Outperforming S&P 500 Prior to Year t	Number of Occurrences	Probability of Outperforming S&P 500 in Year t
1	571	50.4%
2	312	52.0%
3	161	53.4%
4	79	55.8%
5	41	46.4%
6	17	35.3%
7	4	25.0%

Source: Jensen, Michael C., "Risk, the Pricing of Capital Assets, and the Evaluation of Investment Portfolios," *The Business Journal*, Paris 1969.

an entire industry has been formed to provide this information to the public. In fact, fund performance and ratings are available in every library and in all major newspapers on a daily basis. We are overloaded with past performance information, but is the information useful? To answer this question let's look at another study by Michael Jensen. In this study he reviewed the performance persistency of 115 mutual funds from 1955 to 1964.[13] His results are shown in Table 3-1.

Jensen concluded that past performance is not helpful in predicting future performance. Why? Because no matter how many times a fund beat the market in the past, it has about a 50 percent chance of beating the market in the future. These apparently random outcomes are consistent with market efficiency.

In a similar study, Edgar Barksdale[14] and William Green examined the performance persistency of 144 institutional equity managers from January 1975 to December 1989. They ranked the managers based on their results over a five-year period. They then tracked the percentage of these managers that performed better than average in the following five years. Their results show that regardless of where managers place in the first five years, they are about equally likely to be above average as below average in the next five years (see Table 3-2). Again, we see a random pattern that is consistent with the laws of pure chance. You might as well throw a dart at the mutual fund pages in the newspaper. Past performance and mutual fund ratings are of no help in selecting funds that will beat the market in the future.

[13]Jensen, Michael C., "Risk, the Pricing of Capital Assets, and the Evaluation of Investment Portfolios," *Journal of Business* (April 1969), pp. 167–247.

[14]Barksdale, Edgar and William Green, *Pensions & Investments* (September 17, 1990), p. 16.

TABLE 3-2

Institutional Equity Managers' Performance Consistency

Performance Rating for the First Five Years	Percent Finishing in the Top Half the Next Five Years
Top 20%	44.83%
Second 20%	47.67%
Third 20%	51.50%
Fourth 20%	52.33%
Fifth 20%	50.00%

Source: Barksdale and Green

More recently, Ronald Kahn and Andrew Rudd studied the performance of equity mutual funds from January 1983 to December 1993, and fixed income mutual funds from October 1986 to September 1993.[15] They found no evidence of persistence in performance for equity funds and insufficient persistence in fixed income funds to validate their use (because the fixed income funds underperformed their benchmarks by so much). Kahn and Rudd concluded, "Given only past performance information, index funds look best for both equity and fixed income investments."

A major problem of all of these studies is that the underlying data are not free of "survivorship bias." Survivorship bias results when poorly performing funds are dropped from the databases of mutual fund reporting services. For example, Morningstar has data on funds beginning in January 1976, but only on those funds that are still in existence today. Many poorly performing funds have disappeared because they either were closed or merged with other, better performing funds. The absence of data on these funds tends to improve the average results of the survivors. In other words, the performance results of the survivors look better than they really are.

A recent study by Mark Carhart of the University of Southern California looked at the persistency of mutual fund performance after adjusting for survivorship bias.[16] He reviewed the results of all known equity funds from January 1962 through December 1993, including those that did not survive. By December 1993, about one-third of the funds in Carhart's database—the largest and most complete survivor-bias-free database in the world—had disappeared. He concluded that persistence in mutual fund performance is almost totally explained by differences in fund expenses and transaction costs, rather than the superior stock picking or market timing skills of managers. In addition, he found that most funds underperform their benchmarks by the amount of their investment expenses. In his study, actively managed equity mutual funds underperformed index strategies by 1.80 percent per year. Carhart says, "While the popular press will no doubt continue to glamorize the best-performing mutual fund managers, the mundane explanations of strategy and investment costs account for almost all of the important predictability in mutual fund returns."

[15]Kahn, Ronald and Andrew Rudd, "Does Historical Performance Predict Future Performance?" *Financial Analysts Journal* (November-December 1995), pp. 43–51.

[16]Carhart, Mark M., "On Persistence in Mutual Fund Performance," *Journal of Finance* (March 1997), pp. 57–82.

Bond mutual fund results are similar. In a 1993 study conducted by Blake, Elton, and Gruber that examined 361 bond funds beginning in 1977, the authors found that actively managed funds underperformed index strategies by an average of .85 percent per year. In addition, over two-thirds of the funds had negative average excess returns.

Studies of mutual fund performance now span more than 40 years of investigation. The message is clear: *Professional investment managers' efforts to beat the market have failed.* In any asset class, the only consistently superior performer is the market itself.

MARKETS ARE EFFICIENT

If you showed this book to local stockbrokers, they might dismiss our premise, saying, "All they are promising you is market returns. We can show you how to do much better with active management." Unfortunately, they are wrong. It's not their fault; most investment firms still believe in conventional investment wisdom. They do not recognize the significant body of knowledge and empirical evidence that shows that asset class investing significantly outperforms active management strategies in the aggregate.

It is ironic that one of the most competitive sectors of the economy, the financial services industry, is designed to give advice based on the belief that markets do not work. Today, a mind-boggling amount of information is available to professional investors and traders. Reuters alone delivers the equivalent of 27,000 pages of information every second to traders around the globe.[17] All market participants act on their own with significant resources, both capital and information, forcing prices to reflect all known information.

The result of all this competitive activity is that today's price is the best indicator of the value of a stock. The truth is that, as good as Wall Street is at valuing stock given today's information, they can't predict the future. They can't pick individual stocks that will deliver above-average returns, and they can't tell you when the market is going to go up or down. This is not because they are lazy or dumb. It is simply that their best efforts at prediction are rendered ineffective by the invisible hand of free market competition.

For markets to work, prices have to provide accurate signals regarding the allocation of resources. No other pricing system in use in the world today appears better able to allocate resources than the market system. The rest of the world is embracing the theory that markets are efficient, but amazingly, many Americans struggle with the issue. We've witnessed

[17]"Arming for the Data Wars," *The Economist,* June 14, 1997, p. 79.

the fall of the Soviet Union, Eastern Europe, and many other economies that were centrally planned. Their economic failures were due largely to the fact that they were not able to use their resources effectively. Central planning and non-market pricing clearly have not worked.

All you have to do to be a successful information investor is to participate in the free market system and its creation of wealth. You can accomplish this by owning a broadly diversified portfolio of equity securities. This approach works because individual companies attempt to maximize shareholder value. Some of them won't be successful, but on average they will create tremendous wealth for their shareholders.

Don't scan the stock pages to try to find the next Microsoft. You are as likely to pick a loser as you are to pick a winner. Instead, invest in asset class funds that effectively "own the market." Using this approach, you will outperform the majority of those who engage in costly buying and selling.

Even if, despite the overwhelming evidence, you don't believe markets are efficient, you should still follow our advice. Peter Bernstein, the author of *Against the Gods: The Remarkable Story of Risk*, explains why this is so. It boils down to the consequences of being wrong. To summarize, if you believe markets are efficient, you should use asset class funds; if you don't, then you might choose to invest in actively managed funds. The key is to consider what will happen in each case if you are wrong. If you bet that the market is efficient, and it isn't, then you don't give up very much. You still get the above-average returns of a market portfolio. However, if you bet that the markets are not efficient, and they are, you may underperform the market quite badly. In other words, in the attempt to do better, you may do much worse. We feel the risk of betting against the market is too high. Even if the market is not efficient, there is too much that can go wrong using other investment strategies.

SEPARATING SKILL FROM LUCK—THE NATIONAL COIN-FLIPPING CONTEST

Imagine that we are going to hold a national coin-flipping contest beginning tomorrow morning. Exactly 200 million Americans have agreed to participate. Here are the rules:

1. Everyone starts with one silver dollar.
2. You flip your silver dollar once each day as long as you're still in the game.
3. If you flip tails, you lose your silver dollar and you're out of the game.
4. If you flip heads, you keep playing and you share in the pool of all the silver dollars of those who have lost.

On the first day, all 200 million participants flip their coins. Each has a 50 percent chance of flipping heads. We would expect 100 million people to flip heads, stay in the game, and divide up the 100 million dollars of those who flipped tails.

The contest continues for 25 consecutive days. Statistically, at the end of the 25th day we would expect that 6 people have flipped heads 25 times in a row. These champion coin flippers would have accumulated winnings of over 33 million dollars each! They would have overcome tremendous odds and would probably believe they are gifted and skillful coin flippers. The media would have a field day. These six "expert coin flippers" would be invited on national talk shows to describe their secrets of success, and be headlined in newspapers and magazines.

This is a silly story, but it illustrates an interesting point: There is no skill involved in flipping coins—it's just a matter of luck—yet we can see how random luck can be interpreted as skill. We can compare this to the investment world, where fewer professionals beat the market than we would expect to occur simply by random chance. Because there are so many investment managers, some succeed even though their results cannot be distinguished from pure luck. Nevertheless, top performers are recognized as gurus by the press and the investing public.

There is, of course, no conclusive way to prove that successful investment managers are just lucky. But it is hard to dispute the heaps of data that consistently show random variation in manager performance. Like shuffling a deck of cards, the relative performance of investment managers randomly shifts from period to period. If there are uniquely skilled managers out there, we would expect them to demonstrate consistently superior performance; but they do not.

Coin flipping and active management are not games worth playing. Don't get suckered into playing a game of random chance with your hard-earned money, especially when the odds are against you.

4 CHAPTER

Effective Diversification Reduces Risk and Enhances Return

In this chapter, you will learn how to use the first key concept of asset class investing—effective diversification—to reduce risk in your portfolio. Nobel laureate, Merton Miller, when asked to sum up the most important investment concept individuals should know stated, "Diversification is your buddy."

To use effective diversification, you must recognize that markets are indeed efficient. Once you realize that this efficiency exists, you can move on to discover how diversification really works.

AN ISLAND ECONOMY

A brilliant example of diversification comes from Burton Malkiel's book, *A Random Walk Down Wall Street*.[1] Malkiel illustrates the theory in a story about an island economy. On this island are a large resort and a manufacturing firm that makes umbrellas. Naturally, weather affects the fortunes of both. During sunny seasons, the resort does a booming business while umbrella sales plummet. During rainy seasons, the resort owner does very poorly, while the umbrella manufacturer enjoys high sales and large profits.

Table 4-1 shows a hypothetical comparison of the two different businesses during different seasons:

[1]Malkiel, Burton G., *A Random Walk Down Wall Street* (New York: Norton & Company, Inc., 1973).

TABLE 4-1

Seasonal Differences in Returns

	Umbrella Manufacturer	Resort Owner
Rainy Season	50%	-25%
Sunny Season	-25%	50%

Suppose that on average one-half the seasons are sunny and one-half are rainy (i.e., the probability of either a sunny or a rainy season is 50 percent). An investor who buys stock in the umbrella manufacturer earns a 50 percent return half of the time and loses 25 percent of the investment half of the time. On average, the return is 12.5 percent; this is the expected return. Likewise, an investment in the resort produces the same results.

Here's where diversification comes into the story. Suppose the investor puts half the money in the umbrella manufacturing business and half in the resort. Now, during the sunny seasons, a one dollar investment in the resort produces a 50 cent return, while a one dollar investment in umbrella manufacturing loses 25 cents. The investor's total return is 25 cents (50 cents minus 25 cents), which is 12.5 percent of the total investment of two dollars.

The same thing happens during rainy seasons, except that the names are changed. The investment in the umbrella company produces a 50 percent return while the investment in the resort loses 25 percent. Diversification pays off when it either rains all year or is sunny all year. If the investor puts all the money in the resort and it rains all year, the investor has a 100 percent loss. But in our diversified model, a 12.5 percent return is realized nonetheless.

This simple illustration points out the advantage of diversification. Whatever happens to the weather, by diversifying investments across both firms an investor earns a 12.5 percent return each year. The trick is that although both companies are risky (returns are variable from season to season), they are affected differently by the weather. They have a negative covariance. Covariance measures the degree to which two risky assets move in tandem. A positive covariance indicates that asset returns move together, and a negative covariance means they vary inversely. As long as there is some lack of unison in the fortunes of the individual companies in the economy, diversification will always reduce risk.

Portfolios of volatile stocks can be put together in a similar way. The portfolio as a whole can actually be less risky than any one of the individual stocks in it. Low covariance plays a critical role in successful management of institutional stock portfolios. It is the most academically sound approach to reducing risk in your portfolio.

DIVERSIFYING WITH THE U.S. AND JAPANESE EQUITY MARKETS

Consider the case of investing in Japanese stocks. In the early 1990s, the Nikkei index lost more than half of its value, and has not yet recovered from that severe setback. Looking back with the benefit of 20/20 hindsight, we would assume that investment portfolios that stayed out of the Japanese market in that time period would have performed better than those that invested in Japanese stocks. After all, the U.S. market had higher returns with less risk than the Japanese market. A portfolio invested entirely in U.S. stocks would have done a lot better—or would it? Perhaps this time diversification failed. Before you dismiss our theory so quickly, let's examine the data more carefully.

First, let's review the results of a portfolio invested 50 percent in the Standard & Poor's 500 index and 50 percent in a portfolio of U.S. small company stocks. We simulate the performance of this all-U.S. portfolio from January 1, 1983 through December 31, 1997. By the way, this is the best-performing 15-year period in the history of the U.S. market![2] The annualized return for this portfolio is 14.97 percent with a one-year standard deviation of 16.00 percent.[3]

Next, we simulate a similar portfolio of Japanese stocks, consisting of 50 percent Japanese large company stocks and 50 percent Japanese small company stocks. The all-Japanese portfolio has an annualized return of only 10.35 percent with a whopping one-year standard deviation of 34.82 percent! With a lower rate of return than U.S. stocks and much more volatility, how could we possibly advocate diversifying into Japan, especially during this time period?

Here's why. Let's build a third portfolio that is a diversified mix of the first two. This portfolio is invested 75 percent in the all-U.S. portfolio and 25 percent in the all-Japanese portfolio. Here's the point. The diversi-

[2]As measured by the S&P 500 Index.

[3]Assuming the portfolio is rebalanced back to initial target allocations at the end of each calendar year. This is easily done in practice by selling the relative outperforming asset class and buying the relative underperformer.

FIGURE 4-1

A Comparison of Different Portfolios

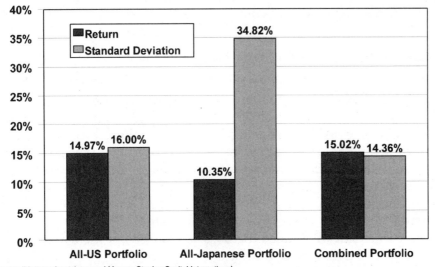

Source: Ibbotson Associates and Morgan Stanley Capital International

fied portfolio's 15.02 percent rate of return is *higher* than either of its components. In addition, the standard deviation drops to 14.36 percent, *lower* than either component. Therefore, although the Japanese market had lower returns and more volatility than the U.S., diversifying with Japanese stocks enhanced returns and reduced risk for a U.S. investor. How is this possible?

The answer is very simple. The low correlation between these markets smoothed out the ride and enhanced overall performance. Purchasing asset classes with a low correlation to one another is the Nobel Prize-winning secret for achieving better portfolio consistency.

What do we mean by low correlation? Correlation is a statistical measure of the degree to which the movements of two variables are related. Measurements range from plus 1.000 (perfect positive correlation) to minus 1.000 (perfect negative correlation). When two assets have a plus 1.000 correlation, they move up and down in the same direction, with the same magnitude. There is no diversification advantage to be gained by pairing two assets with a plus 1.000 correlation. On the other hand, pairing assets having a minus 1.000 correlation would eliminate all risk.

The measurement of correlation and the utilization of asset classes having a low correlation are fundamental ingredients of the asset class investing process. The principle of diversification offers greater comfort to an investor because each asset class follows its own market cycle. In other words, each asset class responds differently to changes in the economy or the investment marketplace. If you own a variety of assets, those that are stable or experiencing a positive return might offset a short-term decline in one asset class. The key is to search out and find groups of investment assets that do not move together.

EFFECTIVE DIVERSIFICATION

While some investors can tolerate the higher risk associated with a lack of diversification, most cannot. Suppose, for example, that all your money is invested in stocks and you need to sell some of your holdings in an emergency. If stock prices are depressed when you need to sell, you might be forced to take a loss. Owning other types of investments would give you more flexibility to raise cash while allowing you to hold your stocks until prices improve. While money market funds provide liquidity and low risk, their overall return is far less than the return from a diversified portfolio. A diversified portfolio provides both liquidity and comparative stability.

Diversification is a prudent method for managing certain types of investment risk. For example, unsystematic risks associated with individual securities can be reduced through diversification. However, it doesn't work if you invest all your assets in the same market segment, or in segments that tend to move in tandem (see Figure 4-2). The risk is that they might all decrease in value at the same time. For instance, investing in the Standard & Poor's 500 Stock index and the Dow Jones Industrial Average would not be effective diversification, because both tend to move in the same direction at the same time. Both indexes are composed of large capitalized companies in the U.S.

FIGURE 4-2

Ineffective Diversification

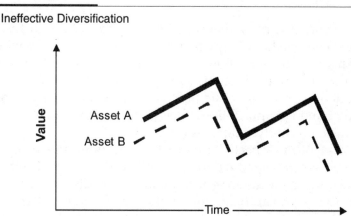

FIGURE 4-3

Effective Diversification

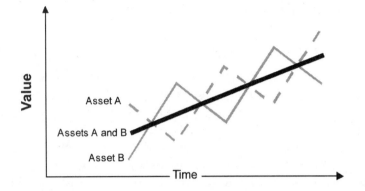

While all diversification is good, certain types of diversification are better. This is the premise of Harry Markowitz's Nobel Prize-winning theory. He shows that, to the extent securities in a portfolio do not move in concert with each other, their individual risks are effectively diversified away (see Figure 4-3). Effective diversification reduces extreme price fluctuations and smoothes out returns. This can best be accomplished through the use of asset class mutual funds.

Over the long term, owning a variety of investments is the best strategy for the investor trying to achieve investment success.

DISSIMILAR PRICE MOVEMENT DIVERSIFICATION ENHANCES RETURNS

A landmark academic discovery that resulted in a breakthrough for investment management methodology can assist you in determining which combination of investments you should own. The discovery is that when two portfolios have the same arithmetic average return, the portfolio with smaller up and down swings in value (less volatility) has a greater compound return. By building a portfolio with asset classes that do not move together, you can significantly reduce its overall volatility.

Consequently, your prospects for a greater compound rate of return over time are improved. This reduction in volatility also allows you to be more comfortable, focus on the long term, and not be distracted by the noise of the day. This is similar to the story of the tortoise and the hare. The hare races like crazy but is out of control, which allows the slow but steady tortoise to ultimately win the race.

IS ONE ASSET CLASS ENOUGH?

We have come through the best 15-year period for stock returns on record in the United States. Extraordinarily good results like this tend to promote a sense of false security among investors. We hear some investors saying, "Based on historical results, I should just put all my money in the S&P 500. I don't need fixed income, and I don't need to diversify." While it is true that stocks have outperformed fixed-income investments over the long run, there have been some *very* long periods of poor performance. This is true of any asset class—they have all had periods of poor performance, and these bad periods are unpredictable. We don't think it is prudent to accept this kind of risk.

Consider Figure 4-4. It shows the decade-by-decade real (after-inflation) returns of the S&P 500 index from January 1930 to December 1997. The average real return is 6.91 percent, but only one decade out of seven is close to average. The returns of the other six decades are significantly higher or lower. Consider how you would have felt in December 1979 after losing an average of 2 percent per year, in real terms, for 10 years. You would have done better if you had invested in Treasury bills. The uncertainty of the returns of individual asset classes is one reason we recommend holding multiple asset categories that are not highly correlated with each other. This should give you more consistent results and help you sleep better at night.

FIGURE 4-4

S&P 500 Index Real Returns

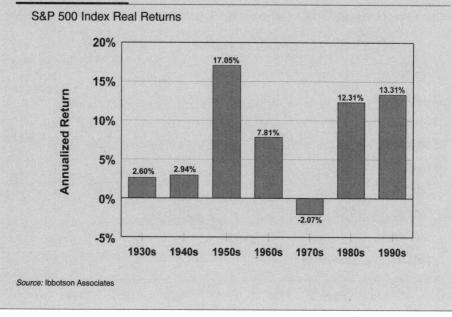

Source: Ibbotson Associates

We have discovered that risk management is one of the keys to investment success. Unfortunately many investors find it difficult to understand. We define effective risk management as the measurement and control of portfolio volatility. By demonstrating how higher portfolio volatility can cause lower rates of return, we hope to create a better understanding of the role of risk in successful investing.

Consider the following hypothetical example. From January 1978 to December 1997, ABC Company stock rises 15 percent each and every year with no variance. The standard deviation of ABC's returns is zero. During the same period, XYZ Company stock also averages 15 percent per year. However, it does so with significant volatility—it has alternating returns of +35 percent and –5 percent. Will ABC and XYZ stocks finish the 20-year period with the same compounded rate of return?

As you can probably guess, the answer is no. Even though they both have an average return of 15 percent, the volatility of XYZ Company stock has cost investors dearly by the end of the twentieth year. The graph below shows the changes to both investment accounts, assuming a $10,000 investment in each stock. The high volatility of XYZ stock has cost its investors $43,280 over this 20-year period. The compound return of ABC stock is 15 percent per year, but the XYZ stock only compounds at 13.25 percent. The lower volatility of ABC stock has created a higher compounded rate of return.

FIGURE 4-5

The Effect of Volatility on the Compounded Rate of Return

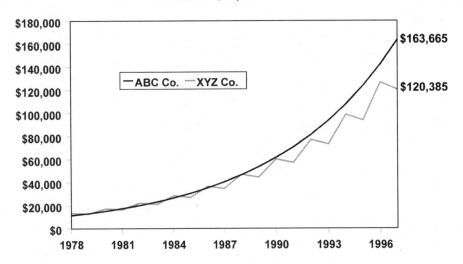

Growth of $10,000

Of course, the complete elimination of portfolio volatility is impossible. But even a small reduction in volatility can create a big improvement in compound returns. You get a big bang for your buck with risk reduction.

This example clearly illustrates the drawbacks of highly volatile portfolios. The next time you're considering two portfolios with similar expected rates of return, you'll know the importance of selecting the one with less volatility. Focusing on portfolio volatility is simply prudent risk management. Lower volatility will improve your wealth as well as increase your level of comfort. This will allow you to more easily sail through inevitable market downturns.

WHY YOU NEED TO REBALANCE

The asset classes in your portfolio will not move in tandem. Therefore, the amount of money you have in each asset category will change as markets fluctuate. In other words, your allocation will drift, much like a sailboat without a rudder. To keep your portfolio on track, we recommend that you periodically rebalance your holdings. This helps you maintain your chosen level of risk, and take advantage of price changes by automatically buying low and selling high.

Here is how rebalancing works. First, you set percentage allocation targets for each asset class in your portfolio. Then you periodically buy and sell to get your portfolio back to its initial target percentages. For example, let's say you have $1,000 invested with $500 in stocks and $500 in bonds (your allocation targets are 50 percent stocks and 50 percent bonds). Let's suppose that one year later your portfolio is worth $1,100 because your stocks went up 15 percent, and are now worth $575, and your bonds went up 5 percent to $525. To maintain your 50/50 target allocation, you need to sell $25 from your stock portfolio and move the money to bonds. This will return your portfolio to the proper 50/50 allocation, $550 in stocks and $550 in bonds. Easy, isn't it?

To illustrate how rebalancing can add value, let's compare the results of two portfolio strategies from January 1969 through December 1997. Both portfolios start with $10,000 of which 30 percent is invested in U.S. large company stocks, 30 percent in international large company stocks, and 40 percent in U.S. Treasury bonds. For simplification, no taxes or transaction costs are assumed. The only difference between the two portfolios is that Portfolio A is rebalanced quarterly, while Portfolio B is never rebalanced.

By December 1997, Portfolio A has a market value of $226,679 while Portfolio B is only worth $215,276. The annual standard deviation of Portfolio A is 5.99 percent compared to 6.51 percent for Portfolio B. In short, Portfolio A delivered higher returns with less risk by rebalancing.

TABLE 4-2

The Effects of Rebalancing

	Portfolio A	Portfolio B
Growth of $10,000	$226,679	$215,276
Annual Standard Deviation	5.99%	6.51%

Source: Ibbotson Associates and Morgan Stanley Capital International

Rebalancing is a simple concept, but realizing the benefits of it is a challenge for most investors. Why? Because it involves selling assets that have recently done well and buying assets that have recently done poorly. It is emotionally difficult to sell winners and buy losers. Our clients often say to us, "Why did you sell the best-performing asset class in my portfolio? I don't want you to sell it, I want you to buy more of it." It is easy to believe that there are trends in the market; to think that what has gone up will continue to go up, and that what has gone down will continue to go down. Unfortunately, investing is not that easy. The market is too efficient for such simple trending to exist. Such trends would be easily exploited and would disappear.

Over long periods, asset class performance tends to be mean reversionary. Periods of above-average returns are often followed by periods of below-average returns—the opposite of a trending market. Rebalancing helps you to take advantage of these cycles and, most important, it keeps you at your chosen level of risk. This is critical risk management because if you never rebalance your portfolio it will become increasingly risky over time. Left unchecked, because stocks outperform bonds in the long run, your portfolio's relative allocation to stocks would increase, making the portfolio inherently more risky.

Proper rebalancing forces you to sell stocks when they are up and buy them when they are down. This sounds counterintuitive and requires a strong sense of discipline and emotional detachment. Most individual investors do the opposite of what they should and it costs them dearly. Consider Stephen Nesbitt's 1995 study of mutual fund results.[4] He concluded that over a 10-year period, not including exit and entry load fees, poor timing errors reduced the returns of retail mutual fund investors by 1.08 percent per year. According to Nesbitt, "Mutual fund cash flows repeatedly go to asset categories near their performance peaks, and leave quickly after returns level off or fall. Poor timing decisions by individuals

[4]Nesbitt, Stephen, *The Journal of Portfolio Management*, Fall 1995, pp. 57-60.

and poor investment decisions by mutual fund managers are together causing a performance shortfall of 2 percent per year or more." Our advice is to use a systematic rebalancing strategy and stick with it. You'll be glad you did.

A RETIREMENT INCOME PORTFOLIO

Let's see how we can use the concept of dissimilar price movement diversification to build a portfolio for retirement income. We do so by simulating the results of a conservative-risk, asset class portfolio from January 1972 to December 1997. The asset mix of the portfolio is shown in Table 4-3. It is globally diversified and is comprised of seven different asset classes. It is invested 50 percent in fixed-income securities and 50 percent in equities.

TABLE 4-3

The Global Conservative Portfolio

Global Conservative Portfolio	Allocation
Cash Equivalents	5%
Two-Year Fixed Income	45%
U.S. Large Companies	18%
U.S. Small Companies	7%
International Large Companies	16%
International Small Companies	6%
Emerging Markets	3%
Portfolio Total	**100%**

For the 25-year period from January 1, 1972 through December 31, 1997, the average annual returns are 6.9 percent for U.S. Treasury bills, 13.3 percent for the Standard & Poor's 500 index, and 13.3 percent for the simulated portfolio. Figure 4-6 shows the growth of $1 invested in these assets. These returns lead us to believe that the safest way to invest so as to provide a steady income with growth is either through a diversified portfolio or the S&P 500, with T-bills far behind. But consider the next eye-opening example that will change your mind.

In Figure 4-7, we assume you invest $100,000 in each of three investment alternatives (Treasury bills, S&P 500, or the diversified portfolio) and that you withdraw $2,000 per quarter from each investment. This is a withdrawal rate of 8 percent of your original investment.

Figure 4-7 shows that Treasury bills present the greatest problem for an income investor because T-bills fail to earn enough to pay out 8 percent per year. The initial investment of $100,000 falls to $31,566—even before adjusting for inflation and taxes! The S&P 500 did better, netting $232,859

FIGURE 4-6

Global Conservative Portfolio vs. S&P 500 and Treasury Bills

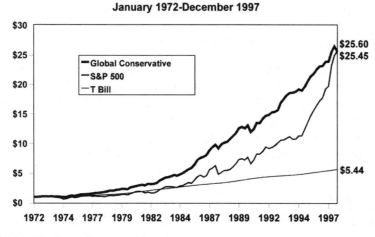

Source: Ibbotson Associates

FIGURE 4-7

Conservative Portfolio vs. S&P 500 and T-Bills Less $2,000 Quarterly Income

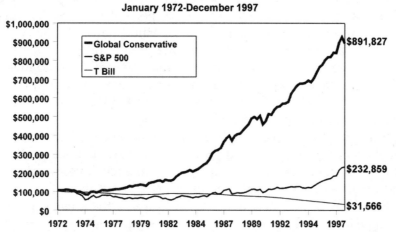

Source: Ibbotson Associates

after removing $208,000 through quarterly distributions. However, the simulated portfolio delivers the best performance by far. After withdrawing the same $208,000, it has an ending balance of $891,827, nearly four times as much as the S&P 500.

Why is there such a dramatic difference between the conservative portfolio and the S&P 500 when their rates of return were fairly close? The answer is that the lower volatility of the conservative portfolio prevents it from being depleted too far in down markets. The severe market declines in 1973–74 cause the S&P 500 to fall much further than the other two investments. The continued income withdrawals during such severe down periods make it very difficult for the account to rebound when the markets recover.

The important message is that *it is critical for income investors to have properly diversified portfolios.* We recommend short-term fixed income securities combined with equity asset classes that don't move together. Being too conservative doesn't work because fixed-income investments do not keep pace with inflation. Being too aggressive doesn't work because the extreme volatility in down markets is too severe. The goal of an investor who needs income should be to optimally combine various asset classes, at an appropriate level of risk, to give the highest expected return. This will help you accumulate wealth steadily while maintaining peace of mind.

MENTAL ACCOUNTING

Investors tend to separate their money into what psychologists call "mental accounts."

Here is an example of how this works.

Imagine that you have decided to go to a concert. As you approach the box office you notice that you have lost the $50 you were going to use to purchase the ticket. Do you use your credit card to buy the ticket anyway? Most people say, "yes." Now consider a slightly different situation. If you had already purchased the ticket and lost it, would you buy another? Most people say, "no."

Why the different answers? Because people allocate expenses to different mental accounts. They place cash in a "general cash account," while a concert ticket already purchased is allocated to a "concert account." People feel they can make up the loss in the cash account by allocating the loss somewhere else. But the lost ticket has already been charged against the concert account. If they were to buy another ticket, the concert account would be charged $100 (two $50 tickets), and that is too much to pay.

FIGURE 4-8

The Mental Accounting Investment Pyramid

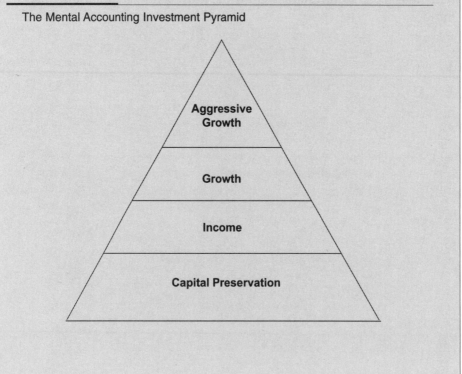

FIGURE 4-9

Asset Class Investing

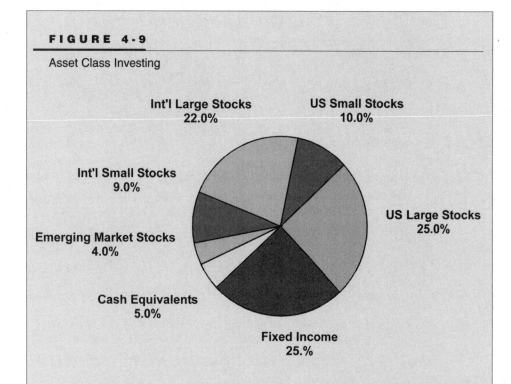

Int'l Large Stocks
22.0%

US Small Stocks
10.0%

Int'l Small Stocks
9.0%

US Large Stocks
25.0%

Emerging Market Stocks
4.0%

Cash Equivalents
5.0%

Fixed Income
25.%

Investors think the same way about their investment assets. They categorize investments by choosing descriptive labels like "aggressive growth," "income," and "capital preservation." Investors feel they are being prudent to allocate some money to safe investments and other money to more aggressive investments. This kind of thinking leads to portfolios that can be depticted by the investment pyramid shown in Figure 4-8.

Unfortunately, allocating your money into mental accounts does not lead to effective diversification because it encourages you to focus on your holdings individually, ignoring the portfolio as a whole and how the pieces interact. You now know that effective diversification is achieved by focusing on the degree to which the returns of different assets in a portfolio are correlated. You want assets that have a low correlation with each other to reduce risk. This means that you have to pay attention to how the different pieces of your portfolio relate to each other. Focusing on asset classes, as depicted in Figure 4-9, does this best.

In Chapter 9, we show you how to build a portfolio using the concepts of effective diversification—expected return, risk, and correlation. The result is a portfolio of asset classes like the one in Figure 4-9.

The Role of Size and Value

Our knowledge of how financial markets work is constantly improving. To maximize your portfolio's performance you have stay on the frontier of financial knowledge. The purpose of this chapter is to share new research with you to further your understanding of how markets work.

So far we have discussed one risk factor for which investors are rewarded: *market risk*. But there are two additional risk factors for which investors are also compensated: *size risk* and *value risk*. The common link between all three risk factors is that they are systematic and cannot be diversified away. They represent common risk factors that are of concern to investors. Because of the higher risk of small stocks and value stocks, there are higher returns available to those investors willing to invest in them. In this chapter, we show you how to incorporate these additional risk factors to add significant incremental return to the performance of your portfolio.

RISK FACTOR 1: MARKET RISK

Market risk is the risk of investing in the equity market as a whole. Investors demand more than the risk-free rate of return to compensate them for the increased risk of holding equities. Market risk cannot be diversified away; everyone who invests in stocks must accept it.

RISK FACTOR 2: SIZE RISK

Small company stocks are stocks of companies with small market capitalization, defined as market price times the number of shares outstanding. Small company stocks carry greater risk than large company stocks because small companies have more limited resources and more variable earnings

FIGURE 5-1

Average Annual Returns 1926–1997

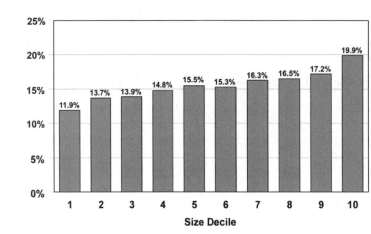

Source: Center for Research in Securities Prices, University of Chicago

than large companies. Small companies are also less able to weather down-turns in the economy. Because of the higher risk of investing in small company stocks, investors demand a higher rate of return for holding them.

Rolf Banz did the original research on size effect in 1981.[1] He discovered that returns increase with decreases in size as measured by market capitalization. We illustrate this phenomenon in Figure 5-1, showing the average annual returns for each size decile from January 1926 to December 1997. Decile 1 stocks are the largest and decile 10 stocks are the smallest. There is a clear relationship between average returns and size—smaller stocks have higher average returns.

It is important to understand that the size effect is not constant. It does not occur every year. It comes and goes at random, and the cycle of good or bad results can last for many years. Consider the period from January 1984 through December 1990 shown in Figure 5-2. During this 7-year period, small stocks dramatically underperformed large stocks. Clearly, betting on small stocks involves risk. It is a risk for which investors are rewarded on average, but only over long periods of time.

RISK FACTOR 3: VALUE RISK

Eugene Fama, working with then fellow University of Chicago professor Kenneth French, began the extensive investigation into the third risk fac-

[1]Banz, Rolf, "The Relationship between Return and Market Value of Common Stocks," *Journal of Financial Economics* (March 1981), pp. 3-18.

FIGURE 5-2

Average Annual Returns 1984–1990

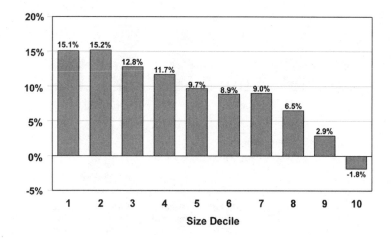

Source: Center for Research in Securities Prices, University of Chicago

tor, commonly known as value.[2] There is no overall agreement on the best way to measure a value stock. Some of the measures used include the price-to-book ratio, price-to-earnings ratio, price-to-cash flow ratio, and dividend yield. Researchers generally agree on the basic characteristics of value stocks: They have low market prices relative to underlying valuation measures, poor earnings growth, and low returns on equity, and they are usually distressed. In essence, they are financially distressed firms that are out of favor with investors. Investors perceive them to be more risky than their successful, healthy counterparts, the growth firms.

Fama and French concluded that value is best identified using the book-to-market (BTM) ratio, which relates the book value of a given company using generally accepted accounting principles with its market value assigned by the stock market. Stocks with high book values relative to their market values are value stocks. Stocks with low book values relative to their market values are growth stocks.

Fama and French found that investors react very differently to companies with different BTM ratios. High BTM companies are hopelessly unpopular with investors; investors demand a higher rate of return to compensate them for the higher perceived risk.

For example, Apple Computer is currently a high book-to-market stock, whereas Microsoft has a low book value relative to its market price. Microsoft stock is the more popular of the two. Why? Because investors

[2]Fama, Eugene F. and Kenneth F. French, "The Cross-Section of Expected Stock Returns," *Journal of Finance* (June 1992), p. 427–465.

FIGURE 5-3

Excellent vs. Unexcellent Company Ratios

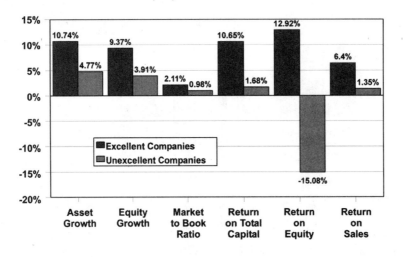

Source: Clayman, M., "In Search of Excellence: The Investor's Viewpoint," *Financial Analysts Journal*, May-June 1987.

expect that low BTM companies like Microsoft will continue to do well, while high BTM companies like Apple will continue to do poorly. Investors want to be compensated for this risk. They are not necessarily looking for a turnaround situation. They simply demand compensation for the possibility that a high BTM company like Apple will do worse than expected or go bankrupt. The market views Apple as a riskier investment.

In order for you to take advantage of this groundbreaking research, you must accept the idea that *you will earn higher rates of return by owning stocks of companies that are doing poorly!*

This is counterintuitive to most investors, but it all comes down to the cost of capital. For example, if you are a banker considering a loan to Apple and Microsoft, to which company are you going to charge a higher interest rate? Apple, of course; it is a more risky investment. Equity investors are also concerned with risk. They too demand higher returns from high BTM companies like Apple. Therefore, stock prices adjust to reflect the perceived riskiness of Apple stock.

There are thousands of stockbrokers and analysts who spend their professional lives trying to identify great companies that you should own. If only you could build a portfolio of the best-performing companies, wouldn't you be assured of investment success?

Michele Clayman raises this question in an article based upon the best-selling book *In Search of Excellence* by Peters and Waterman.[3] Clayman tracks

[3]Clayman, Michele, "In Search of Excellence: The Investor's Viewpoint," *Financial Analysts Journal* (June 1987), p. 63.

the performance of both the excellent companies described in the book, as well as companies from the group who are truly unexcellent in the same performance areas. She examines several traditional business ratios and finds that, on average, the excellent companies have much higher ratios than the unexcellent companies. Figure 5-3 summarizes her findings.

Figure 5-4 shows the cumulative return that investors would have received if they had invested $100 in two portfolios, one made up of all the excellent companies and the other consisting of all the unexcellent companies. Contrary to your intuition, *the unexcellent companies significantly outperform the excellent companies.* This higher stock performance is explained by the value risk factor.

Like all risk factors, value delivers higher returns in the long run, but not always in the short run. It does not work in each and every period; it requires a long time horizon. You must be willing to suffer through some periods of underperformance if you want to gain the benefits of value investing over the long haul. To illustrate, consider a second study conducted by Clayman in 1994.[4] In this study Clayman found that, from 1988 to 1992, the unexcellent companies underperformed the excellent companies. Clearly, value investing is not a sure thing in the short run. Another consideration is that a portfolio of pure value stocks might be heavily weighted toward stocks of specific industries like banking, financial services, or manufacturing. Such a portfolio would be very sensitive to economic shocks like unexpected inflation or interest rate increases.

[4]Clayman, Michele, "Excellence Revisited," *Financial Analysts Journal* (May-June 1994), pp. 61–65.

FIGURE 5·4

Unexcellent Companies Outperform Excellent Companies

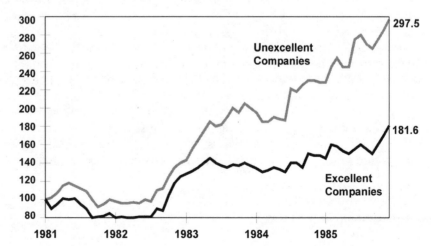

Source: Clayman, M., "In Search of Excellence: The Investor's Viewpoint." *Financial Analysts Journal,* May-June 1987, p. 63.

BEHAVIORAL FINANCE AND VALUE STOCKS

Modern finance theory generally does not address behavioral explanations of investor behavior. It views investors as rational decision makers who behave logically. In the case of value stocks, the standard finance view is that the higher returns of value stocks exist to reward rational investors for taking more risk.

Economists who follow the ideas of an emerging new discipline called behavioral finance take a different view. They believe that cognitive errors lead investors to think erroneously that *good stocks* are stocks of *good companies*.[5] But in reality, we know that *good stocks* (stocks with higher expected returns) are stocks of *bad companies* (companies with high BTM ratios, or value stocks).

Behavioral finance economists believe the two common cognitive errors that investors make are due to "representativeness" and the "pain of regret." Representativeness leads investors to think that growth stocks are good stocks to own because they represent what investors believe successful companies, with good stock returns, look like. Good companies like Microsoft look like they should deliver good stock returns in the future, as they have done in the past. Investors ignore empirical evidence that shows there are fewer growth stocks that do well than value stocks that do well. In other words, they overestimate the probability that a growth stock will be a good investment. A rational investor does not make decisions this way. A rational investor studies historical evidence and concludes that growth stocks have lower expected returns and, therefore, value stocks are a better investment.

The pain of regret partially explains the higher returns of value stocks, especially among institutional investors. To illustrate, let's assume you are a money manager for a pension fund and you hold a portfolio of conventional growth stocks—stocks of companies like Microsoft that are popular and performing well. If your portfolio does poorly, you can justify your choices by showing how highly rated, popular, and financially strong the companies are. You were just unlucky; your portfolio's poor perfomance was an act of God. Besides, if your portfolio is widely diversified, it won't underperform the market by too much anyway. If, however, you hold a portfolio of value stocks and the portfolio does poorly, you will have to face an angry board of trustees with little ammunition to justify your choices. You constructed a portfolio of out-of-favor, poorly rated stocks, and it did not pay off. If you hold extreme value stocks you might dramatically underperform the market and risk losing the account. The pain of regret makes value stocks hopelessly unpopular among institutional investors. They don't want to risk holding a portfolio of "dogs" that is different from competitors' portfolios and the market as a whole.

Although the rational finance and behavioral finance explanations of value are different, both come to the same conclusion: *Value stocks have higher expected returns than growth stocks.* Whether you believe the higher returns are from higher risk, cognitive errors, or a combination of the two, value stocks should be part of your portfolio.

---

[5]Shefrin, Hersh and Meir Statman, "Making Sense of Beta, Size, and Book-to-Market," *Journal of Portfolio Management* (Winter 1995), pp. 26–34.

THE LONG-TERM RESULTS OF VALUE INVESTING

In this section we define value stocks by their BTM ratios. The BTM ratio is a simple and effective way of capturing the value dimension of risk. We start by dividing all 1,650 NYSE-listed companies into 10 equal groups based on their respective book-to-market ratios. Next, we add American Stock Exchange and National Market OTC issues to the NYSE decile groupings. We have excluded from the chart companies that do not have available book value data, such as American Depository Receipts, closed-end issues, or negative book value firms.

Stocks in the first through third deciles are considered low BTM stocks or growth stocks. Stocks in the eighth through tenth deciles are considered high BTM stocks or value stocks. For example, Berg Electronics Corp. has the lowest BTM ratio of all companies on the NYSE, .012 on December 31, 1996. This means that its book value is only 1.2 percent of its current market capitalization. It is clearly a growth stock. Potlatch Corporation, on the other hand, represents the opposite end of the spectrum. Its book value is 98.7 percent of its market capitalization. It is a value stock.

In Figure 5-5, we show the performance of both high BTM stocks and low BTM stocks for both large and small companies. Large company stocks are defined as those stocks in the first through fifth deciles based on market capitalization, and small company stocks are defined as the sixth through tenth deciles. The benchmark portfolio for large companies is the S&P 500. The benchmark for small company stocks is the CRSP 6-10 Index, which corresponds to the bottom half of the U.S. market based on market capitalization.[6]

[6] Center for Research in Securities Prices at the University of Chicago.

TABLE 5-1

Book-to-Market Deciles

Book-to-Market Deciles	BTM (Decile Lowest)	NYSE Name	NYSE	AMEX	NASDAQ
1	162,790	Berg Electronics Corp.	165	66	533
2	7,096	Cardinal Health Inc.	165	24	323
3	3,273	SBC Communications	165	29	290
4	1,938	Fluor Corp.	165	39	249
5	1,175	Fisher Scientific Inc.	165	32	244
6	784	Barnes Group Inc.	165	34	301
7	527	Helmerich & Payne Inc.	165	52	318
8	352	Personell Group Amer.	165	47	344
9	201	CTS Corp.	165	71	395
10	95	Potlatch	165	116	542

The 1,650 companies on the New York Stock Exchange are divided into 10 equal deciles based on book-to market. American Stock Exchange and National Market OTC issue are put into the NYSE decile groupings. Decile breaks as of December 31, 1996

Source: Dimensional Fund Advisors, Inc.

The Role of Size and Value

FIGURE 5-5

Historical Returns 1964–1997

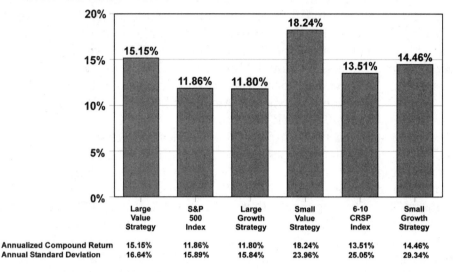

	Large Value Strategy	S&P 500 Index	Large Growth Strategy	Small Value Strategy	6-10 CRSP Index	Small Growth Strategy
Annualized Compound Return	15.15%	11.86%	11.80%	18.24%	13.51%	14.46%
Annual Standard Deviation	16.64%	15.89%	15.84%	23.96%	25.05%	29.34%

Data courtesy Fama-French. Value and Growth include hold ranges and estimated trading costs. April 1993–Present: Dimensional Fund Advisors Value Mutual Fund Portfolio net of all fees

Note that the standard deviations are roughly the same for stocks in a given size category, irrespective of their BTM ratio. However, high BTM stocks produce a higher average annual return. In fact, high BTM stocks as a group produce about 4 percent higher annual returns with the same standard deviation as low BTM stocks. Clearly, the market views risk as something more than just volatility of returns. Financial distress and poor performance are also risk factors of concern to investors. Therefore, investors require higher rates of return for investing in poor performers. The specific risk of owning a single high BTM stock is significant. However, owning *all* the high BTM stocks, through a diversified asset class portfolio, produces volatility that is similar to owning all the stocks in the market. We feel that this is the best way to capture the higher returns of value stocks.

INTERNATIONAL VALUE STOCKS

Is value risk rewarded internationally? Yes, it is. A 1993 study by Carlo Capaul and Ian Rowley, conducted in conjunction with Stanford University's William Sharpe, supports and supplements Fama and French's findings in the domestic market.[7] Capaul, Rowley, and Sharpe show not only that an

---

[7]Capaul, Carlo, Ian Rowley, and William F. Sharpe, "International Value and Growth Stock Returns," *Financial Analysts Journal* (January-February 1993), pp. 27–36.

international high BTM stock portfolio outperforms global market indices, but also that the excess returns are greater on average than those found in the United States. These excess returns, combined with the low correlation of returns between countries, make foreign value portfolios especially attractive to U.S. investors.

Building an international high BTM portfolio presents many challenges, the most important of which is how to cope with the varying foreign accounting rules. Fortunately, we are only interested in capturing the relative BTM risk factor in each country. Therefore, we do not have to compare accounting standards between countries. The same screening process used in the U.S. market can be used in each foreign market.

Fama and French compare the relative performance of an international high BTM asset class portfolio to both Morgan Stanley's Europe-Australia-Far East (EAFE) Index and a low BTM portfolio. The higher returns are dramatic, as shown in Figure 5-6. The annual difference in returns between high and low BTM portfolios is 5.6 percent. The annual difference in returns between high BTM portfolios and the EAFE Index is 4.9 percent. These results are just too significant to ignore. Investors should build their portfolios to gain access to this higher return asset class.

FIGURE 5·6

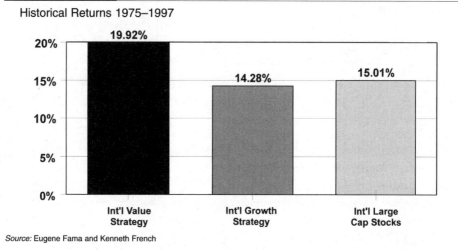

Historical Returns 1975–1997

Source: Eugene Fama and Kenneth French

6 CHAPTER

Asset Class Mutual Funds—
The New Paradigm

$\mathcal{I}$n this chapter, we show you the most effective tool available today for implementing your asset class investing strategy. Many years ago when we first began offering our investment strategies to clients, we had to use retail mutual funds. Unfortunately, we found significant structural problems with these funds. Now we have better tools—we call them asset class mutual funds.

WHAT ARE ASSET CLASS MUTUAL FUNDS?

Asset class mutual funds deliver the investment results of an entire asset class—a group of securities with similar risk and expected return characteristics. Asset class funds are best used as building blocks in creating efficient portfolios and in achieving dissimilar price movement diversification. They are usually only available to institutional investors such as pension funds, banks, and insurance companies, or to clients of fee-only registered investment advisors.

The four most important attributes of asset class mutual funds are:

1. low operating expenses,
2. low turnover,
3. low trading costs, and
4. consistent asset allocation.

1. Low Operating Expenses

You should only consider investing in mutual funds that are true no-load funds. They should have no front- or back-end loads, redemption fees, or 12b-1 marketing expenses. All mutual funds, including no-loads, have operating expenses. These expenses include management fees, administrative charges, and custody fees, and are expressed as a percentage of assets. The average annual expense ratio for all retail equity mutual funds is 1.54 percent.[1] In comparison, the same ratio for asset class funds is typically only about one-third of that. Other factors being equal, lower costs lead to higher rates of return. Therefore, the lower cost structure is a big advantage for asset class funds.

An important study of retail equity mutual funds by Elton and Gruber showed that there is an inverse relationship between cost and performance.[2] In addition to showing that retail equity funds as a whole underperform the market, Elton and Gruber found that the more expensive a fund is, the worse it performs on average.

Elton and Gruber measure performance using a statistic called alpha, which is simply a measure of risk-adjusted performance relative to the overall market.[3] If a fund's alpha is negative, it has underperformed the market after adjusting for risk. The lower the alpha, the worse the fund did. Notice that for each category of operating expenses in Table 6-1, all the alphas are negative and the worst funds are those with the highest expenses. Low expenses is one of the main reasons we use asset class mutual funds in all of our client portfolios.

2. Low Turnover

Active mutual fund managers do a lot of trading, thinking this adds value. As a result, the average retail mutual fund has a turnover rate of 83 percent.[4] This means that 83 percent of the securities in the portfolio are trad-

---

[1]This was calculated by screening the Morningstar database as of December 31, 1997 for the average total operating expense ratio of all equity mutual funds. On that date there were 4,967 equity mutual funds.

[2]Elton, Edwin J., Martin J. Gruber, Sanjiv Das, and Matthew Hlavka, "Efficiency with Costly Information: A Reinterpretation of Evidence from Managed Portfolios," *The Society for Financial Studies* (1993).

[3]The difference between the expected and actual rates of return on a mutual fund is called alpha, which shows the excess returns the mutual fund earned above the market.

[4]This was calculated by screening the Morningstar database as of December 31, 1997 for the average turnover of all equity mutual funds. On that date there were 4,967 equity mutual funds.

TABLE 6-1

Relationship of Alphas and Expense Ratios

Expense Ratio			Alpha
91%	to	202%	-3.87
75%	to	91%	-1.68
68%	to	75%	-0.69
59%	to	68%	-1.19
0%	to	59%	-0.59

ed on average over a 12-month period, representing $83,000 of traded securities for every $100,000 invested.

High turnover is costly to shareholders because each time a trade is made there are transaction costs involved, including commissions, spreads, and market impact costs. These hidden costs may amount to more than a fund's total operating expenses if the fund trades heavily or if it invests in small company stocks whose trading costs are very high.

Why do retail mutual funds have such high turnover rates? Because their managers are under tremendous pressure to perform. Good short-term performance leads to a bonus for the manager and a flood of new money for the fund. If the funds are performing poorly, managers often try to make up ground by changing the composition of their holdings.

In addition, fickle investors can cause excess turnover. Fickle investors are retail investors who chase after performance. They move in and out of mutual funds trying to find hot markets or managers. This forces fund managers to buy and sell more often than they would prefer. Unfortunately, fickle investors do not pay their fair share of the transaction costs they create. They are allowed to buy and sell at net asset value, effectively free-riding on the backs of buy-and-hold, long-term investors.[5] You should avoid funds with high turnover rates as well as those that attract fickle investors by advertising heavily.

Elton and Gruber also studied the effects of turnover on mutual fund performance (see Table 6-2).[6] Not surprisingly, they found an inverse relationship between turnover and performance; the higher the turnover, the worse the performance. Fortunately, asset class mutual funds have extremely low turnover rates, usually less than 25 percent per year. This keeps transaction costs low and improves returns.

[5]Some funds, especially those that invest in markets that lack liquidity, are beginning to use back-end charges to discourage investors from moving money in and out so quickly.

[6]Elton et al., "Efficiency with Costly Information."

Relationship Between Alphas and Turnover

Turnover Rate			Alpha
72%	to	162%	-2.21
51%	to	72%	-1.87
34%	to	51%	-2.17
22%	to	34%	-1.11
0%	to	22%	-0.58

Taxes

If a mutual fund sells a security for a gain, it must make a capital gain distribution to shareholders because mutual funds are required to distribute 98 percent of their taxable income each year, including realized capital gains, to stay tax-exempt at the corporate level. They distribute all their income annually because no mutual fund manager wants to have his or her performance reduced by paying corporate income taxes.

Two recent academic studies examined the extent to which capital gains distributions reduce after-tax returns on mutual funds. These studies demonstrate that tax efficiency is an important factor to consider in selecting equity mutual funds.

In one study, Stanford University economists John B. Shoven and Joel M. Dickson found that taxable distributions have a negative effect on the rates of return of many well-known retail equity mutual funds.[7] Shoven and Dickson measured the performance of 62 equity funds for the period from January 1963 to December 1992. They found that a high tax bracket investor who reinvested after-tax distributions ended up with an accumulated wealth per dollar invested of *only 45 percent* of the funds' published performance. An investor in a middle tax bracket realized just 55 percent of published performance.

In another study, Robert H. Jeffrey and Robert D. Arnott concluded that low portfolio turnover can be a factor in improving a fund's after-tax performance.[8] Jeffrey and Arnott compared the performance of large, actively managed equity mutual funds with a passively managed equity index fund from January 1982 to December 1991. They found that only 21 percent of the funds, 15 out of 72, outperformed the index fund on a pretax basis. *Only 7 percent of the funds*, 5 out of 72, outperformed the index

[7]Shoven, John B. and Joel M. Dickson, "Ranking Mutual Funds on an After-Tax Basis," Stanford University Center for Economic Policy Research Discussion Paper (#344).

[8]Jeffrey, Robert H. and Robert D. Arnott, "Is Your Alpha Big Enough to Cover Its Taxes?" *Journal of Portfolio Management* (Spring 1993).

CHAPTER 6

fund after taxes were considered. Clearly, it is very difficult for a mutual fund to add value through active management, especially on an after-tax basis. Jeffrey and Arnott concluded that, "Passive indexing is a very difficult strategy to beat on an after-tax basis and, therefore, active taxable strategies should always be benchmarked against the after-tax performance of an indexed alternative."

There is yet another tax problem associated with actively managed funds, which became evident during the stock market crash of 1987. After the crash, many mutual fund managers cleaned house and sold many stocks that had appreciated during the bull market of the early 1980s. This resulted in higher than normal turnover rates for the year, and very large capital gain distributions for shareholders. For example, if you had invested $100,000 in Fidelity Magellan on December 31, 1986, you would have lost 8.7 percent of your principal as of December 31, 1987. However, despite the loss, Magellan made capital gain distributions during the year. If you were in the 20 percent tax bracket, you would have owed $1,057 in capital gains taxes even though your account declined in value, adding insult to injury.

3. Low Trading Costs

Trading costs are composed of commissions, bid–ask spreads, and market impact costs. While trading costs are much greater for smaller stocks than for larger stocks, they can be significant for both. In the case of small-cap stocks in particular, trading costs can exceed management fees.

For an example, let's examine a trade that a mutual fund might execute in the over-the-counter market. If the spread on a stock is 5 percent, say $10 ask and $9.50 bid, the manager would have to buy it at the ask for $10 and sell it at the bid for $9.50. This results in a $0.50 cost, assuming no market impact, which represents a 5 percent cost of trading. If 80 percent of the portfolio turns over during the year, this amounts to a total hidden annual cost of 4 percent (80 percent times 5 percent).

Trading costs increase significantly when you invest in smaller companies. To calculate this effect we need to define a range of sizes. As of December 1996, there were 1,920 domestic operating companies on the NYSE. In Table 6-3, we divide these companies into 10 equal groups of 192 stocks, based on market capitalization, which is defined as market price times shares outstanding. We then allocate American Stock Exchange and NASDAQ issues to these size categories.

General Electric is the largest company listed on the NYSE with a market capitalization of over $162 billion. The largest company in the tenth decile is Harborside Healthcare Corporation, with a market size of only

TABLE 6-3

Allocation of American Stock Exchange and NASDAQ to NYSE

Market Capitalization Deciles	Size ($MM)	NYSE Largest Company	Number of Companies		
			NYSE	AMEX	NASDAQ
1	162,790	General Electric Company	192	1	18
2	7,096	Federated Dept. Stores	192	2	30
3	3,273	Dow Jones & Co.	192	6	55
4	1,938	BJ Services Co.	192	7	83
5	1,175	Federal Signal Corp.	192	5	116
6	784	Heilig Meryers Co.	192	12	175
7	527	Zilog Inc.	192	20	240
8	352	Marcus Corporation	192	31	430
9	201	Coopers Cos. Inc.	192	92	787
10	95	Harborside Healthcare	192	391	1895

Size is Defined by NYSE Market Capitalization Deciles
Market Capitalization = Price x Shares Outstanding
Data as of 12/31/96

Source: Ibbotson Associates

$95 million. Difference in size is a significant factor in the cost of trading. The smaller the market capitalization, the higher the trading costs (see Table 6-4).

The bid–ask spread as a percentage of price is a conservative estimate of actual trading costs. The spreads in the smallest decile are nearly 12 times greater than in the largest decile. An investor purchasing at the ask and selling at the bid would pay trading costs of 0.53 percent for the largest stocks and 6.19 percent for the smallest stocks, if they do not move the market. A large trade—one that is a significant percentage of the daily trading volume for a security—is likely to influence the price, thus adding additional costs to the transaction.

As a rule of thumb, you can estimate the trading costs of a mutual fund by multiplying its turnover rate by the bid–ask percentage spread for the size decile of its average holding. For example, consider a mutual fund with an average market capitalization in the fifth decile that has a turnover rate of 86 percent. We would estimate that this fund has a 1.08 percent hidden cost of trading (.86 percent X 1.25 percent = 1.08 percent). This hidden cost is in addition to published expenses. All of these costs drag down the fund's performance. For international funds the situation is worse, because trading costs are higher in foreign markets.

TABLE 6-4

Size Difference Significance in Cost of Trading

Size Decile	Average Price	Percent Spread	Daily Trading Volume Per Issue	
			Shares	Dollars
1	$53.92	0.53	904,445	$47,294,212
2	$42.70	0.60	506,539	$19,300,213
3	$38.19	0.71	336,778	$10,772,236
4	$33.12	0.98	211,360	$5,354,680
5	$27.32	1.25	164,897	$3,697,177
6	$25.79	1.26	117,658	$2,645,244
7	$22.87	1.61	88,745	$1,636,101
8	$19.16	2.21	60,099	$846,424
9	$14.84	2.99	37,894	$415,914
10	$8.35	6.19	17,462	$119,256

**The smaller the market capitalization, the higher the potential trading costs
and the smaller the daily volume**

Source: Bridge (February 1, 1996)

4. Consistent Asset Allocation

Most investment advisors agree that the largest determinant of performance is asset allocation—how money is divided among different asset
categories. However, you can only accomplish effective asset allocation if
the mutual funds in your portfolio maintain consistent asset allocation.
That is, the funds you use need to stay within their target asset classes.
Unfortunately, most actively managed funds change their asset class exposures over time. Equity funds, for example, may change their composition by moving across size or value dimensions and sometimes even
across different markets, such as from domestic to international securities.
In addition, most funds increase or decrease their cash balances based on
cash flow conditions and market fluctuations. This can significantly
change the overall allocation of your portfolio.

In effect, if you use these funds you have relinquished control of your
asset allocation to the managers of the mutual funds. The managers do not
know the particulars of your situation; therefore, they make allocation decisions based on their needs rather than yours. Fortunately, asset class
funds as well as pure index funds consistently maintain their market segment exposures. This keeps you in control of your allocation.

To illustrate this concept, we compare the asset class consistency of two popular funds, Fidelity Magellan and Vanguard's S&P 500 Index, from August 1981 through March 1997 (see Figures 6-1 and 6-2). You can see that Magellan's allocation has dramatically changed over time, whereas the Vanguard S&P 500 Index has stayed relatively constant. Using a fund like Magellan that changes its asset class exposure makes it impossible to know the exact allocation of your overall portfolio. To solve this problem, you should use asset class funds. Then you won't have to worry about them deviating from their targets and throwing off your overall allocation.

Unfortunately, asset class investing has not been adequately exposed to retail investors. Very few asset class funds, or even pure index funds, are sold directly to retail investors. Since management fees on these funds are far less than on traditional funds, it is unlikely that many mutual fund sponsors will be offering these funds any time soon.

However, several progressive mutual fund families do offer retail index mutual funds to the public. We list them in Table 6-5.[9]

THE NEW INVESTMENT PROFESSIONAL

In Chapter 12 we show you how to build your own portfolio using asset class mutual funds, a good place to get started if you have less than $100,000 to invest. If you have a larger amount to invest, it might make sense to work with a qualified fee-only advisor.

Many excellent fee-only advisors around the country use institutional asset class funds in managing client portfolios. These advisors allow their clients to gain access to institutional mutual funds that otherwise would not be available to them. In Chapter 13 we discuss how to select one of these professionals.

Most asset class fund managers work exclusively with institutional clients, typically large pension plans with billion-dollar portfolios, and do not make their funds available to the public. However, they do make their funds available to the clients of approved investment advisory firms, so you can gain access to these funds if you are a client of an approved firm. This will enable you to enjoy the same cost structure and investment strategies as some of the largest institutions in the country.

[9]This was calculated by screening the Morningstar Database as of December 31, 1997 for all non-institutional index mutual funds.

FIGURE 6-1

Fidelity Magellan Exposure Distribution

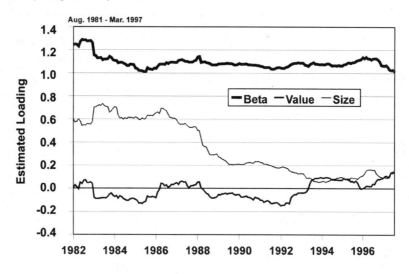

There are two reasons why these funds are so restrictive. First, they are simply not equipped to handle direct public investment. They don't have the personnel to answer customer phone calls, the facilities to handle thousands of transactions and statement mailings each month, or the bud-

FIGURE 6-2

Vanguard Index 500 Exposure Distribution

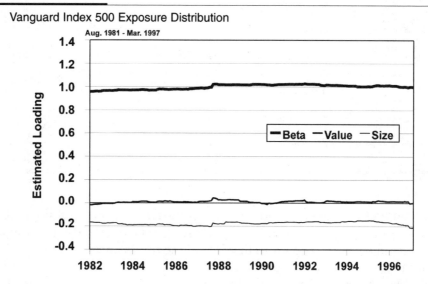

TABLE 6-5

Retail Index Mutual Funds

Fund Name	Investment Objective	Fund Incept Date	Fund Family	Phone Number
AARP U.S. Stock Index	Growth and Income	97-02	AARP Investment Program	800-322-2282
American Cent Global Gold	Specialty--Prec Metals	88-08	American Century Investments	800-345-2021
American Cent Global Nat Res	Specialty--Nat Res	94-09	American Century Investments	800-345-2021
American Gas Index	Specialty--Nat Res	89-05	Rushmore Group	800-343-3355
ASM Index 30	Growth and Income	91-03	ASM Fund	800-445-2763
BT Adv EAFE Equity Idx Adv	Foreign Stock	96-06	BT Funds	800-730-1313
BT Adv Small Cap Index Adv	Small Company	96-08	BT Funds	800-730-1313
BT Adv US Bond Index Adv	Corp Bond--General	97-07	BT Funds	800-730-1313
BT Investment Equity 500 Idx	Growth and Income	92-12	BT Funds	800-730-1313
California Invmt S&P 500 Idx	Growth and Income	92-04	Calif. Investment Trust Gp.	800-225-8778
California Invmt S&P MidCap	Growth	92-04	Calif. Investment Trust Gp.	800-225-8778
California Invmt S&P SmC Idx	Small Company	96-10	Calif. Investment Trust Gp.	800-225-8778
Dreyfus Intl Stock Index	Foreign Stock	97-06	Dreyfus Group	800-645-6561
Dreyfus MidCap Index	Growth	91-06	Dreyfus Group	800-373-9387
Dreyfus S&P 500 Index	Growth and Income	90-01	Dreyfus Group	800-373-9387
Dreyfus Small Cap Stock Idx	Small Company	97-06	Dreyfus Group	800-645-6561
Federated Max-Cap Instl	Growth and Income	90-07	Federated Funds	800-341-7400
Federated Mid-Cap	Growth and Income	92-11	Federated Funds	800-341-7400
Federated Mini-Cap	Small Company	92-09	Federated Funds	800-341-7400
Fidelity Spartan Market Idx	Growth and Income	90-03	Fidelity Group	800-544-8888
Galaxy II Large Co Index Ret	Growth and Income	90-10	Galaxy Funds	800-628-0414
Galaxy II Small Co Index Ret	Small Company	90-10	Galaxy Funds	800-628-0414
Galaxy II U.S. Treas Idx Ret	Govt Bond--Treasury	91-06	Galaxy Funds	800-628-0414
Galaxy II Utility Index Ret	Specialty--Utilities	93-01	Galaxy Funds	800-628-0414
Gateway Mid-Cap Index	Growth	92-09	Gateway Group	800-354-6339
Gateway Small Cap Index	Small Company	93-06	Gateway Group	800-354-6339
Green Century Equity	Growth and Income	95-09	Green Century Funds	800-934-7336
Key Stock Index	Growth and Income	96-07	Key Mutual Funds	800-539-3863
Merrill Lynch Aggregate Bd A	Corp Bond--General	97-04	Merrill Lynch Group	609-282-2800
Merrill Lynch Intl Index A	Foreign Stock	97-04	Merrill Lynch Group	609-282-2800
Merrill Lynch S&P 500 Idx A	Growth and Income	97-04	Merrill Lynch Group	609-282-2800
Merrill Lynch Sm Cap Idx A	Small Company	97-04	Merrill Lynch Group	609-282-2800
Northern Stock Index	Growth and Income	96-10	Northern Funds	800-595-9111
Norwest Advant Index I	Growth and Income	94-11	Norwest Advantage Funds	800-338-1348
Prudential Bond Market Idx Z	Corp Bond--General	97-10	Prudential Dryden Fund	800-225-1852
Prudential Stock Index Z	Growth and Income	92-11	Prudential Mutual Funds	800-225-1852
Schwab 1000 Inv	Growth and Income	91-04	Schwab Funds	800-435-4000
Schwab International Idx Inv	Foreign Stock	93-09	Schwab Funds	800-435-4000
Schwab S&P 500 Inv	Growth and Income	96-05	Schwab Funds	800-435-4000
Schwab Small Cap Index Inv	Small Company	93-12	Schwab Funds	800-435-4000
Strong Index 500	Growth and Income	97-05	Strong Funds	800-368-1030
T. Rowe Price Equity Index	Growth and Income	90-03	Price T. Rowe Funds	800-638-5660
U.S. Global Inv All Amer Eq	Growth and Income	81-03	U.S. Global Investors	800-873-8637
USAA S&P 500 Index	Growth and Income	96-05	USAA Group	800-382-8722
Vanguard Balanced Index	Balanced	92-09	Vanguard Group	800-662-7447
Vanguard Bond Idx Intrm-Term	Corp Bond--General	94-03	Vanguard Group	800-662-7447
Vanguard Bond Idx Long-Term	Corp Bond--General	94-03	Vanguard Group	800-662-7447
Vanguard Bond Idx Short-Term	Corp Bond--General	94-03	Vanguard Group	800-662-7447
Vanguard Bond Idx Total	Corp Bond--High Quality	86-12	Vanguard Group	800-662-7447
Vanguard Index 500	Growth and Income	76-08	Vanguard Group	800-662-7447
Vanguard Index Extend Mkt	Small Company	87-12	Vanguard Group	800-662-7447
Vanguard Index Growth	Growth	92-11	Vanguard Group	800-662-7447
Vanguard Index Sm Cap Stk	Small Company	60-10	Vanguard Group	800-662-7447
Vanguard Index Tot Stk Mkt	Growth and Income	92-04	Vanguard Group	800-662-7447
Vanguard Index Value	Growth and Income	92-11	Vanguard Group	800-662-7447
Vanguard Intl Eqty Emerg Mkt	Diversified Emerg Mkts	94-05	Vanguard Group	800-662-7447
Vanguard Intl Eqty European	Europe Stock	90-06	Vanguard Group	800-662-7447
Vanguard Intl Eqty Pacific	Pacific Stock	90-06	Vanguard Group	800-662-7447
Vanguard Special REIT Index	Specialty-Real Estate	96-05	Vanguard Group	800-662-7447

get to conduct a large-scale advertising program. Second, public availability would attract hot money and the problems associated with it that we discussed earlier. The bottom line is that the funds' institutional clients will not permit them to accept direct public investment. Involving public shareholders would significantly increase costs and disrupt the funds' ability to keep cash flow and turnover rates low.

WHICH ASSET CLASSES SHOULD YOU USE?

Now that you know about asset class mutual funds, which ones should you use? A good starting point is to review the historical performance of each asset category you are considering. This is not to say that the past indicates future performance; it does, however, indicate reasonable relationships between the long-run returns and risk of various asset classes.

Time series data on domestic asset classes are available starting in 1926. The data include periods of major crises as well as boom times. Think of all the social, political, and economic events of the last eight decades. How did the markets perform through all this turmoil and change?

Looking at Figure 6-3, you can see that equities have far outperformed fixed income securities. If you had invested $1 in the Standard & Poor's 500 Index on January 1, 1926, it would be worth $1,829 (assuming reinvestment of dividends) at the end of 1997. One dollar invested in small company stocks would be worth an incredible $4,738!

In contrast, fixed income investments barely beat inflation. That same $1 investment in 20-year U.S. government bonds would be worth only $39, and in 30-day Treasury bills only $14. Compare the results to the fact that a $1 investment over this period required an increase in value of $9 simply to maintain purchasing power. You need to have growth above the rate of inflation to make money in real terms. Fixed investments deliver little return above inflation.

FIGURE 6-3

Stocks, Bond, Bills, and Inflation

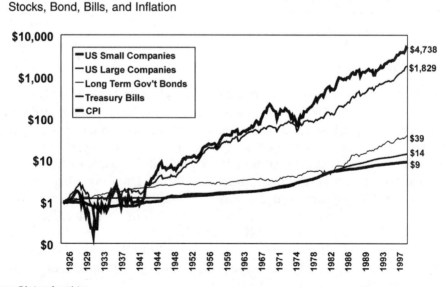

Source: Ibbotson Associates

Table 6-6 shows a series of returns for different time periods. In each period, the S&P 500 index returns more than both long-term U.S. government bonds and inflation. During most periods, long-term U.S. government bonds barely exceeded inflation. Even in the years during which government bonds substantially beat the inflation rate, the S&P 500 performs better than both.

Table 6-7 shows the inflation-adjusted or real returns for several different 15-year periods. Stocks dominated bonds in all periods. Moreover, even in the period ending in 1980 when all three assets have negative real returns, the equities declined the least. In fact, stocks only recorded one negative 15-year period, while Treasuries and corporate bonds each recorded two.

TABLE 6-6

Nominal Annualized Total Returns

Number of Years	Time Period	S&P 500	L.T. Gov't Bonds	Inflation (CPI)
72	1926-97	11.0%	5.2%	3.1%
50	1948-97	13.1%	5.7%	4.0%
40	1958-97	12.3%	6.7%	4.5%
30	1968-97	12.1%	8.7%	5.4%
20	1978-97	16.6%	10.5%	4.9%
10	1988-97	18.1%	11.5%	3.5%
5	1993-97	20.2%	10.5%	2.7%

Source: Ibbotson Associates

TIME HORIZON

Financial theory suggests that equities should have higher expected returns than fixed income investments because of their greater volatility. Volatility is of greatest concern to investors who anticipate the need to liquidate their investments in the near future. If you are a long-term investor, it is prudent to invest a portion of your portfolio's assets in equities because short-term volatility is of no consequence. The percentage of equities you should have in your portfolio depends on many factors such as age, health status, return objectives, income stability, risk tolerance, and employment situation, among other things.

The minimum time horizon to invest in equities should be at least 5 years, but preferably 10 years or more. Any money with less than a 5-year horizon should be invested in fixed income instruments. We suggest that

TABLE 6-7

Real Annualized Returns

	Real (Inflation Adjusted) Annualized Returns For Fifteen-Year Periods Ending in...						
	1997	1996	1995	1990	1980	1970	1960
S&P 500 Index	14.1%	10.9%	13.2%	9.8%	7.7%	(-0.5%)	10.1%
LT Corp. Bonds	8.2%	9.4%	9.9%	6.5%	3.6%	(-3.9%)	(-1.9%)
30 Day T-Bills	2.7%	3.2%	2.9%	2.9%	2.2%	(-0.6%)	(-2.0%)

Source: Ibbotson Associates

you view the investment process as part of a long-term financial plan, because the range of annual returns is significant for equity asset classes, but is reduced over longer periods.

FIXED-INCOME ASSET CLASSES

Fixed-income securities form an important part of a comprehensive portfolio because they provide stability to counterbalance the high volatility of equities. While they have lower expected returns than stocks, they add value to a portfolio by reducing overall volatility. Bonds are the primary tools for pinpointing your portfolio to your target risk level. A higher allocation of bonds reduces portfolio risk and a lower allocation of bonds increases portfolio risk.

A bond represents a loan to an issuer, such as the U.S. government or a major corporation, usually in return for periodic fixed interest payments. The payments continue until the bond is redeemed at maturity (or earlier if called by the issuer). At the time of maturity, the investor receives the face value of the bond. Bonds with maturities of less than 5 years are considered short term, those with maturities between 5 and 12 years are intermediate term, and bonds with maturities longer than 12 years are long term.

Many investors buy long-term bonds because they normally have higher current yields than shorter-term bonds. Investors consider them safe, but in reality long-term bonds carry many different kinds of risk, including reinvestment risk, call risk, purchasing power risk, liquidity risk, and interest rate risk.

The major risk you face with long-term bonds is interest rate risk. Because prices of bonds move in the opposite direction of interest rates, when rates rise, prices of bonds fall, and vice versa. For example, consider a newly issued 20-year Treasury bond with a 6 percent coupon. If over the next 12 months interest rates increase by 2 percent, new 20-year Treasury bonds will be offered with 8 percent coupons. Therefore, the old 6 percent bonds will be worth less than the new bonds, because the new bonds have higher coupons. This illustrates how falling interest rates force bond prices up. Alternatively, interest rates might rise and force bond prices down. The inverse relationship between interest rates and bond values is an important risk of fixed-income investments. It can create significant volatility, especially for long-term bonds.

To give you an idea of the volatility of long-term bonds, we show the historical rates of total return of 20-year Treasury bonds over seven decades in Figure 6-4. During the 1980s, long-term bond investors enjoyed one of the best decades ever, with gains averaging 12.7 percent per year. Bond prices soared during this decade due to declining interest rates. Because of these high returns, long-term bonds became very popular in the late 1980s and early 1990s, reflecting the fact that investors often mistakenly place too much importance on their most recent experiences. Psychologists call this cognitive bias. We call it rearview mirror investing: It's like trying to drive a car by looking through the rearview mirror. We believe it is critical to analyze all the statistical evidence that is available when making financial decisions.

Now consider the decade of the 1950s, the worst decade for long-term bond investors. It shows an average annual return of *negative* 0.1 percent including reinvested interest. Here we see what can happen to long-

FIGURE 6-4

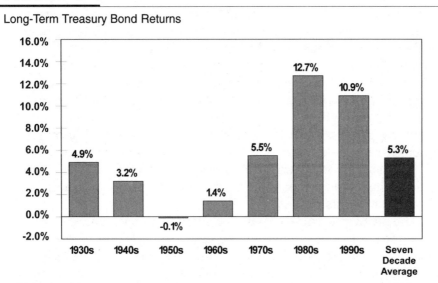

Long-Term Treasury Bond Returns

Source: Ibbotson Associates

CHAPTER 6

FIGURE 6-5

Risk and Reward Examined for Bonds

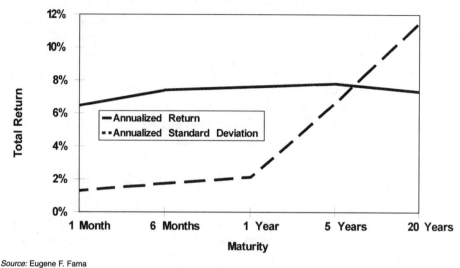

Source: Eugene F. Fama

term bond returns when interest rates rise. Most investors don't realize that the volatility of long-term bonds is close to the volatility of common stocks. The data show that long-term bonds don't provide the low level of risk that many fixed-income investors seek.

The higher risk of long-term bonds would be acceptable if investors were sufficiently rewarded with higher rates of return. Eugene Fama of the University of Chicago studied the rates of return of long-term bonds from 1964 to 1997. He found that the term premium for longer-term bonds is not reliable.[10] His research, which has been updated in Figure 6-5, shows that long-term bonds have wide variances in their rates of return and, most important, that bonds with maturities beyond five years don't offer sufficient reward for their higher risk.

The predominant investors in the long-term bond markets are institutions such as corporate pension plans and life insurance companies. These investors are interested in funding long-term obligations, including fixed annuity payments or other fixed corporate responsibilities. In general, they are not concerned with volatility of principal or with the effects of inflation because their obligations are fixed in maturity date and amount. You, on the other hand, should be concerned with inflation as well as volatility, be-

[10]Fama, Eugene F., "Time Varying Expected Returns," unpublished paper (February 1988, data updated regularly).

cause you are an individual living in a variable rate world. There is a limit to the amount of volatility with which you can feel comfortable.

We believe you should own fixed-income investments to provide stability to your portfolio, but not to generate high returns. High returns should come from equities. Fixed-income securities can help offset the risk of your equity holdings and, therefore, lower the risk of your overall portfolio. You can accomplish this best by using short-term fixed-income securities rather than long-term bonds. Short-term bonds have less volatility and a lower correlation to stocks, and are a better choice for your portfolio. They will allow you to invest a larger percentage of your money in stocks while maintaining low portfolio risk.

Bond Funds: Asset Class Funds versus Pure Index Funds

Pure index funds that invest in bonds attempt to replicate the performance of a predetermined index. This is usually done through full or partial replication of the underlying index. Asset class funds, on the other hand, have the flexibility to add value through trading strategies.

One such strategy involves examining the current shape of the yield curve to determine the choice of maturity. This approach is based on research that shows the current yield curve is the best estimate of future yield curves.[11] The yield curve is a graphical summary of market yields for different maturities. Estimating future yield curves enables asset class fund managers to calculate the expected horizon returns and determine optimal maturity and holding periods. This is a purely objective approach with no subjective forecasting involved.

As an example of this technique, consider an asset class fund that is limited to securities with maturities of two years or less. The manager extends maturities when there is a reward for doing so (when the yield curve is steep as in Figure 6-6), and holds short maturities when longer maturities do not provide additional expected return (when the yield curve is flat or inverted as in Figure 6-7).

Following this approach, the manager constructs a matrix of expected returns like the one shown in Figure 6-8, and then determines the optimal maturity and holding period. In the example in Figure 6-8, the highest expected return is 9.73 percent. This return is achieved by buying a fixed instrument with a maturity of 18 months, and selling it 3 months later when it has 15 months to maturity.

This investment strategy is called matrix pricing, and has been developed by leading financial economists at the University of Chicago. It serves as the core strategy of several asset class funds that we use for our clients. In studies as well as in live results, it has added 50 to 100 basis

[11]Ibid.

FIGURE 6-6

Determining Optimal Maturities

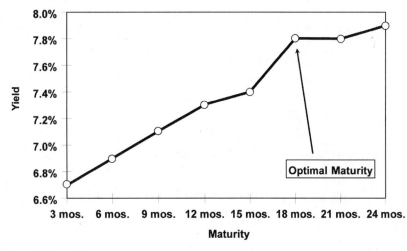

Source: Dimensional Fund Advisors

FIGURE 6-7

Determining Optimal Maturities

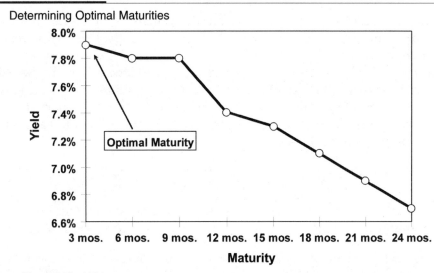

Source: Dimensional Fund Advisors

FIGURE 6-8

Matrix of Expected Returns

Maturity (months) at Time of Sale	24	21	18	15	12	9	6	3
21	8.65							
18	8.32	7.98						
15	8.79	8.85	9.73					
12	8.50	8.45	8.68	7.64				
9	8.39	8.32	8.44	7.80	7.95			
6	8.22	8.13	8.17	7.65	7.65	7.35		
3	8.07	7.98	7.98	7.54	7.51	7.29	7.22	
0	7.90	7.79	7.76	7.37	7.30	7.08	6.94	6.66

Maturity (months) at Time of Purchase

Source: Dimensional Fund Advisors

points more than comparable pure index funds annually over extended periods. For our clients, we use two different asset class funds. The first is a high-quality, two-year corporate fund. The second is a two-year U.S. government fund. Both funds use the matrix pricing strategy.

EQUITY ASSET CLASSES

As we discussed earlier, equities offer the potential for higher returns. This, of course, comes with higher risk. According to the Fama and French research, three dimensions of risk—market, value, and size—explain the majority of stock returns.[12] Value stocks and small stocks have higher expected returns and higher risk than growth stocks and large stocks, respectively. Therefore, value stocks and small stocks should be part of your asset class portfolio. We recommend that you use the following value and small company asset classes.

Value Stocks

Fama and French define value stocks as the stocks of companies ranked in the highest three deciles (the top 30 percent) of book-to-market ratios. This

[12]Fama, Eugene F. and Kenneth F. French, "The Cross-Section of Expected Stocks Returns," *Journal of Finance* (June 1992), pp. 427-465.

CHAPTER 6

is an extreme definition of value that captures the effect of the value dimension of returns. There are publicly available indexes that also attempt to capture the value dimension. However, these indexes define value as those companies ranked in the top half (the top 50 percent) of book-to-market ratios. We feel these indexes do not capture the value dimension of returns as completely as Fama and French do. Data suggest that a more extreme definition of value results in higher expected returns. Therefore, we suggest you use asset class funds that define value as the top three deciles of book-to-market ratios. This will give you full exposure to high-expected-return value stocks.

Small Company Stocks

Small company stocks not only have higher expected returns than large stocks; they also have a low correlation. In Table 6-8, we illustrate the dissimilar price movements between large and small stocks by dividing the equity market into ten equal deciles. The left-hand column shows three-year rolling periods from 1929 to 1997. We have shaded the highest and lowest returning deciles for each three-year period. Notice that the shaded boxes are concentrated at the extremes of the market—the largest stocks and the smallest stocks. This means the most extreme movements, good or bad, usually occur in large company stocks and small company stocks and that there is a low correlation between these two asset classes.

To maximize diversification, we recommend that you use an asset class fund that invests in deciles nine and ten. These deciles have the lowest correlation with large stocks. In addition, they have the highest expected returns. Building a portfolio of asset classes with a low correlation results in greater long-term performance, while reducing risk through diversification.

Equity Funds: Asset Class Funds
versus Pure Index Funds

Most pure index funds that invest in small-cap stocks track the Russell 2000 Index. The securities in this index fall primarily in deciles six through eight. These index funds buy all or most of the securities in the index in proportionate market weights. Their goal is to match the index with as little tracking error as possible. Instead of a retail Russell 2000 index fund, we use an institutional asset class fund that invests in deciles nine and ten. This fund is not restricted to holding a portfolio that mirrors the exact market-weighted composition of the 9-10 index. Instead, it is free to add value through a sophisticated discount block trading strat-

TABLE 6-8

NYSE Decile Annualized Returns (%)

Time	1	2	3	4	5	6	7	8	9	10
1929-31	-26.79	-33.06	-35.65	-36.69	-37.13	-39.94	-40.56	-44.77	-49.31	-49.70
1932-34	10.61	23.85	28.86	29.73	20.19	31.19	27.63	41.35	41.23	60.76
1935-37	8.18	9.19	2.30	4.19	8.67	5.36	10.56	3.58	12.48	8.75
1938-40	6.09	4.18	7.06	8.38	12.48	12.87	9.73	8.42	2.44	-8.47
1941-43	7.81	15.31	14.89	15.83	16.79	16.48	24.75	30.31	33.47	55.46
1944-46	13.14	20.83	20.04	24.01	26.64	27.15	25.85	28.90	35.59	38.61
1947-49	9.07	8.24	8.13	6.80	6.35	5.48	3.56	3.85	2.70	4.61
1950-52	21.39	22.71	19.15	20.93	19.15	20.16	21.50	21.80	18.59	18.39
1953-55	24.38	22.12	22.88	20.60	22.74	24.38	21.46	20.77	22.80	24.74
1956-58	10.63	15.09	13.04	15.57	14.92	10.70	15.41	14.45	15.26	13.18
1959-61	12.49	13.20	15.98	14.39	14.44	13.44	14.41	13.82	14.32	12.76
1962-64	8.25	6.73	6.65	5.63	2.63	3.73	5.13	5.33	3.63	4.46
1965-67	5.96	10.85	16.40	19.58	22.86	25.18	26.15	30.20	33.33	39.51
1968-70	1.26	1.83	3.27	-2.30	0.04	0.41	-4.36	-3.70	-6.39	-3.05
1971-73	7.21	0.82	-0.33	-0.33	-3.60	-3.54	-5.58	-7.42	-10.65	-10.01
1974-76	4.19	11.62	13.04	15.90	14.56	14.77	17.16	20.01	19.55	22.46
1977-79	4.60	8.63	13.38	16.87	19.79	22.82	25.25	25.05	27.75	34.74
1980-82	13.46	17.36	19.00	20.06	20.91	22.18	20.17	20.57	20.16	19.41
1983-85	19.06	20.53	18.34	16.96	17.23	19.04	19.52	18.32	16.87	11.94
1986-88	12.32	13.30	13.20	13.04	11.13	8.23	8.39	6.79	3.08	0.74
1989-91	19.43	16.48	18.01	16.52	14.85	13.40	14.44	9.39	8.43	2.26
1992-94	4.62	8.26	9.35	9.07	13.50	12.46	13.02	9.43	11.17	18.31
1995-97	32.49	28.17	25.79	25.97	20.91	24.22	27.16	23.64	26.84	22.85

Source: Ibbotson Associates

egy and a willingness to be slightly overweighted or underweighted, relative to its benchmark, on any particular stock. This allows the fund to manage the high trading costs involved in such small, illiquid stocks. In fact, the fund has had negative buy-side trading costs every year since 1987.[13]

Here is an example of how it works (see Figure 6-9). The major shareholder of a small company wants to sell 351,000 shares, or 3.2 percent of the company. The company's market capitalization is $106 million, and its average daily trading volume for the previous month is 15,600 shares. Before the trade, the last sale occurred at 9 5/8, with the current bid at 9 5/8 and the ask at 9 3/4. The shareholder agrees to sell shares in one big block to the fund at 9 3/8, below both the ask price of 9 3/4 and the bid price of 9 5/8. The trading cost to the fund is negative 3.9 percent. In other words, the fund made money on the trade.

Why would a shareholder sell at such a discounted price? The shareholder needed liquidity and was willing to pay for it. An attempt to sell such a large block through normal channels would have driven down the

[13]Documented by Professor Donald Kiem of the Wharton Business School.

FIGURE 6·9

An Example of a 9-10 Trade

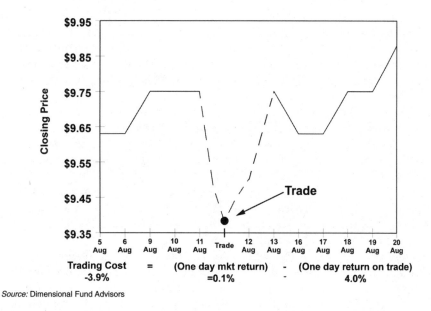

Trading Cost = (One day mkt return) − (One day return on trade)
-3.9%   =0.1%   −   4.0%

Source: Dimensional Fund Advisors

market price significantly, probably much lower than the price at which the sale to the fund took place.

A discount block trading strategy like this allows an asset class mutual fund to more fully capture the higher returns of small company stocks. It helps to reduce the large trading costs normally associated with such small, illiquid stocks. Through these enhancements, managers of asset class mutual funds can achieve a comparative advantage for their clients.

THE RATING GAME

Do you remember the 1970s television show *The Dating Game*, whose contestants tried to identify the right person to take on a date? A contestant would ask a few simple, usually embarrassing questions of three contestants of the opposite sex that were seated behind a wall. The three hidden contestants tried through their answers to make a good enough impression to be chosen for a date.

The mutual fund rating game works in much the same way. Investors use ratings of mutual funds that are listed in newspapers and magazines as a guide to help them pick funds that are right for their portfolios. Choosing an A-rated fund is a quick and easy way to choose a fund, but are these ratings useful?

Let's consider the mutual fund ratings in the *Wall Street Journal* that are compiled by Lipper Analytical Services. Lipper awards an A to funds whose returns rank in the top 20 percent of their category. The next 20 percent get a B, and so on through C, D, and E.

Here is a sample of the ratings for the period ending December 31, 1997. For the five-year period the Vanguard Index 500 fund is awarded an A, the highest rating possible, while the Vanguard Index Small Company fund is only worth a C. This means that the Vanguard Index 500 fund is ranked in the top 20 percent of similar funds, and the Vanguard Index Small Company fund only ranks in the middle of its peer group. Likewise, for the last three years the Vanguard Index European fund merits the highest rating of A, while the Vanguard Index Pacific fund only gets a D, and for the previous 12 months the Vanguard Index Emerging Markets fund is stuck with an E—the worst rating possible.

Something is very odd—and very wrong—with these ratings. All of these funds are pure index funds. They simply track the performance of a predetermined market index. How can one fund deserve an A rating while another is only worth only a D or an E?

Index funds have low costs and are widely diversified, so they should consistently rank modestly above average compared to other funds in their peer group. Accordingly, they deserve no better and no worse than a B rating. The only possible explanation for the Lipper ratings is that the Vanguard funds are not benchmarked properly—they are not matched to their correct peer groups.

This is surprising, because index funds should be the easiest of all mutual funds to rank. They simply mirror broad market segments and disclose exactly what's in their portfolios. Actively managed funds are much harder to classify than index funds because they have changing styles, moving asset allocations, and other complications. If Lipper can't classify index funds correctly, how accurate can its other ratings be?

Mutual fund managers know that the ratings game is being played and how important it is for their funds to get good ratings. Good ratings bring money into the funds and bonuses to the managers. Naturally, managers try to do whatever they can to improve their ranking. For example, a recent study by Keith Brown, Van Harlow, and Laura Starks found that mutual fund managers increased the risk level of their portfolios around the middle of the year if they were not ranked among peer group performance leaders.[14] If they were successful and their fund's ranking improved, the managers would get bonuses and the fund would get increased assets from investors. If the gamble failed, the fund performed worse than it would have if they had not made any changes. But because mutual funds are a winner-take-all industry, fund managers feel it is a worthwhile gamble to take. Unfortunately, they are playing performance games with your money!

The mutual fund rating game is a loser's game. Don't play it. Use asset class funds and ignore the mutual fund ratings published by the financial press.

[14]Brown, Keith, Van Harlow, and Laura Starks, "On Tournaments and Temptations: An Analysis of Managerial Incentives in the Mutual Fund Industry," *Journal of Finance* (March 1996), pp. 85-110.

Adding Value through Global Diversification

In this chapter, you will learn how to lower risk and increase returns using international asset classes in your portfolio—the fourth key concept of asset class investing. Global diversification has become an industry standard among U.S. institutional investors and has long been a tradition among investors in Europe and Asia. The popularity of international investing among individual investors in the U.S. is growing, but international investing still represents only a small portion of total U.S. investment assets.

Unfortunately, most individual investors still view foreign equity investments suspiciously, even though the empirical evidence for such diversification is compelling. Let's examine the benefits of international investing, including how the markets work and which international asset categories should be part of your asset class portfolio.

Would you limit your investments to only one industry or one state? Of course not. Doing so would dramatically limit your investment opportunities and diversification benefits. Intuitively you know that you should diversify across a wide variety of companies that are located in different geographical areas and compete in different industries. International diversification is simply an extension of this idea to the international markets. Global investing allows you to gain dimensions of risk control and reward that are not available in the U.S. markets.

Today, many of the world's capital markets are equal to U.S. markets in sophistication, liquidity, and safety. The foreign securities markets are massive. For example, in 1989 the world's government bond market capitalization was over \$6 trillion, with nearly half of it overseas (Figure 7-1).[1]

---

[1]"How Big Is the World Bond Market? 1990 Update," a monograph of the International Bond Market Analysis (New York: Salomon Brothers, 1990).

FIGURE 7·1

World's Government Bond Market Capitalization

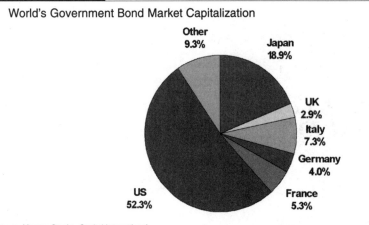

Source: Morgan Stanley Capital International

In 1970, the total value of the world's equity markets was slightly below $511 billion and U.S. equities made up 68 percent of the total value (Figure 7-2). But by 1996, just 26 years later, the world equity markets had risen to over $10 trillion in value and the U.S. share had declined to 43 percent (Figure 7-3).[2] Although the U.S. market has increased in size since 1970, it has not grown nearly as quickly as the equity markets of the rest of the world.

Once you accept the fact that international diversification makes sense, you must decide which international asset classes to include in your portfolio. Let's review the three major candidates for inclusion: international fixed income, international equity, and emerging market asset classes.

INTERNATIONAL FIXED-INCOME ASSET CLASSES

The fixed-income component of your portfolio is intended to mitigate risk. When the equity markets decline, fixed-income securities will dampen the fall. Therefore, we feel you should only hold short-term, high-quality, and highly liquid securities. Many foreign government bond markets—including the markets of Japan, the United Kingdom, Switzerland, the Netherlands, Germany, and France—meet these criteria. They have credit quality equal to the U.S. according to debt ratings by Moody's and Standard & Poor's.

[2]Morgan Stanley Capital International.

FIGURE 7-2

1970 Market Capitalization

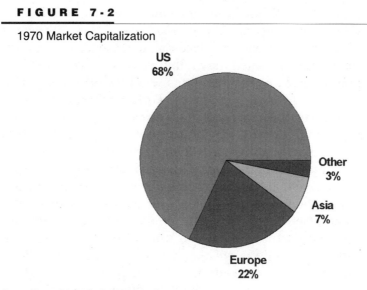

Source: Morgan Stanley Capital International

FIGURE 7-3

1997 Market Capitalization

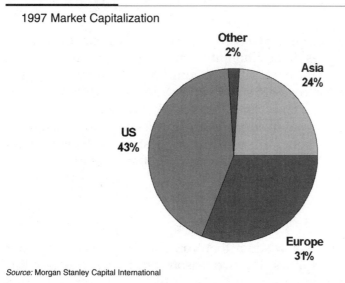

Source: Morgan Stanley Capital International

But there's a catch. If you purchase bonds denominated in a foreign country's currency, you not only take on the risks associated with bonds themselves, you also accept currency risk: the risk that the foreign currency in which the bond is denominated may fall in value relative to the U.S. dollar. If that happens, your overseas holdings will be worth less in U.S. dollar terms and your return will be reduced. Fortunately for investors, currency risk can be hedged away using foreign currency forward contracts. Hedging is a technique of investing in an asset with a return pattern that offsets your exposure to a particular source of risk. Because currency risk is such a large component of the overall risk of international fixed-income securities, we believe that hedging must be done in this asset class.

Table 7-1 includes data from 1987 to 1993 for the fixed-income markets of Canada, France, Germany, and Japan. When both hedged and unhedged equally balanced portfolios of similar duration are compared, we find that the unhedged portfolio is twice as volatile as both the hedged portfolio and domestic fixed-income alternatives. Hedging must be done because the risk associated with the unhedged portfolio is too great.

TABLE 7·1

Risk Measures of Fixed Income Strategies (1987–1993)

	Global Hedged*	Global Unhedged*	Five-Year Treasury Index	Lehman Gov/Corp Index
Standard Deviation (%)	4.05	9.01	4.57	4.68
Duration	5.55	5.55	4.37	5.34

Standard Deviation Annualized from Monthly Data
Equal Weighted Portfolio of Lehman Country Indices: US, UK, Japan, France, Germany and Canada

Unfortunately, hedging can be costly, especially if you are exposed to many different currencies. In addition, it is impossible to create a perfect hedge unless you know the exact value of your holdings at the end of the hedging period. It is also costly to run an international fixed-income fund due to custodial expenses, taxes, and duty fees. For these reasons, we do not recommend international fixed-income securities as part of your asset class portfolio. Foreign bonds have a low correlation with other asset classes, but we feel the higher costs of investing in them mitigate their diversification benefits.

INTERNATIONAL EQUITY ASSET CLASSES

It has become conventional wisdom that you should put some of your money in international equities. The two reasons most often given for this recommendation are that foreign stocks have historically outperformed

U.S. stocks and that foreign stocks provide good diversification due to their low correlation with U.S. markets. While it is true that international stocks continue to provide good diversification and low correlations with the U.S., the higher returns of international stocks are a myth. The recent rally in the U.S. market has wiped out the return advantage once held by foreign markets. For the period January 1969 to December 1997, Morgan Stanley Capital International's EAFE Index has returned 12.13 percent per year, while the S&P 500 has returned 12.16 percent. Furthermore, foreign market returns have been improved by currency gains versus the dollar. Even in 1994, before the big run-up in U.S. stocks, the returns of foreign and domestic stocks were about equal in local currency terms (see Table 7-2).[3]

The fact that U.S. and international stock returns have been about the same should not surprise you. It is consistent with financial theory that the expected returns of equivalent risk securities, no matter where they are located in the world, should be the same. Investments of equal risk, and firms with equal costs of capital, should have the same expected returns. Put in another way, a company like Honda should be no more risky for a Japanese investor than General Motors is for an American investor. This is especially true today, when capital can be raised so easily anywhere in the world. Large firms in some countries like Israel have an easier time issuing securities outside their borders. There is simply no reason for a company in Europe to have a higher cost of capital than a similarly capitalized company of equal risk in the United States. We believe that companies of equal size that are located in major developed markets are considered equally risky by the market and, therefore, are priced to yield the same expected return. Actual market returns confirm that our view is correct.

Rather than investing in international equities for higher returns, *you should include them in your portfolio to reduce risk.* The international and U.S. equity markets have a low correlation; they do not tend to move together. Figure 7-4 shows that international diversification affects the trade-off be-

---

[3]Sinquefield, Rex, "Where Are the Gains from International Diversification," a manuscript for Dimensional Fund Advisors, April 4, 1995.

TABLE 7-2

Returns of Foreign and Domestic Stock (1970–1994)

	S&P 500	EAFE ($US)	EAFE (Local)
Compound Return	10.97	13.21	10.52
Standard Deviation (Risk)	15.90	23.35	20.35
Arithmetic Mean	12.13	15.48	12.42

Source: Sinquefield, Rex, "Where Are the Gains from International Diversification," a manuscript for Dimensional Fund Advisors, April 4, 1995.

FIGURE 7-4

January 1970–December 1997

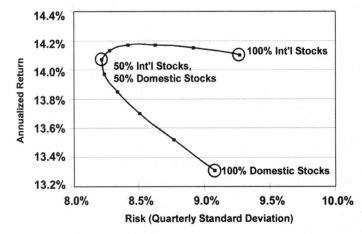

Source: Ibbotson Associates, Morgan Stanley Capital International.

tween risk and return. It illustrates the different risk–return relationship for different mixes of U.S. and international stocks.

The higher a point is on the chart, the higher the return; the further to the left a point is, the lower the risk. We illustrate that, from January 1970 through December 1997, investors achieved a higher rate of return with less volatility by owning international stocks in addition to U.S. stocks. The graph shows different combinations of two portfolios, one domestic and one foreign, each with 70 percent in large stocks and 30 percent in small stocks. Each circle represents a different combination of the two portfolios using 10 percent increments (e.g., 100/0, 90/10, 80/20, etc.). The optimum portfolio during this time period—the portfolio delivering the highest return relative to risk assumed—occurs when 50 percent of the portfolio is invested in domestic stocks and 50 percent in foreign stocks. This 50/50 portfolio also had the least volatility. The exact amount of international exposure that is right for you depends on many factors, including your comfort level with foreign holdings and your willingness to have results that differ from U.S. markets. As a guideline, we recommend that you have a minimum of 30 percent and a maximum of 60 percent of your equities invested in well-diversified foreign stocks.

Most international asset class funds and pure index funds have portfolios that are market-capitalization weighted. In other words, the fund manager allocates money to countries based on the sizes of their markets, measured by market capitalization. Currently, Japan is the largest market outside the United States. Therefore, a market-capitalization weighted international fund will allocate more money to Japan than to any other country.

We believe this approach puts too much money in Japanese stocks. The overweighting occurs because in Japan it is common for companies to invest in the stocks of other companies.[4] These cross holdings are counted twice, overstating the market capitalization of Japan relative to the rest of the world. In the institutional asset class fund we use for our investors, Japan's weighting is limited to 38 percent to compensate for this effect. You should do the same in your portfolio.

[4]Ibid.

CAN YOU GAIN INTERNATIONAL DIVERSIFICATION BY OWNING THE STOCK OF A U.S. MULTINATIONAL COMPANY?

Why not just buy the stocks of U.S. multinational firms to get global diversification? After all, many U.S. multinationals get more than half their earnings from overseas operations. It *seems* safer and more convenient to get international exposure this way, but we don't recommend it. The stocks of multinational firms tend to follow the movements of their local markets rather than those of the international market. This is true regardless of the degree to which their operations are globally diversified. For example, Figure 7-5 compares the returns of Colgate-Palmolive, Inc. with the S&P 500 Index over the last five years. Colgate gets about 80 percent of its revenues from foreign operations, yet its stock price still closely followed the U.S. market during a period when foreign markets significantly underperformed. Because stocks of U.S. multinational firms are so highly correlated with the U.S. market, they lose their diversification power. To capture the diversification benefits of foreign equities, you must purchase shares of companies headquartered in foreign countries.

FIGURE 7-5

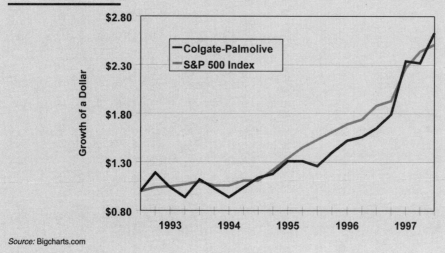

Source: Bigcharts.com

ARE INTERNATIONAL MARKETS EFFICIENT?

Many U.S. managers argue that the international markets are not efficient. This logic assumes that local investors in foreign countries can't figure out the correct prices for their securities. For some reason, American managers think they can sit at a desk in New York and value German companies more accurately than a German banker in Munich can. They believe they can take advantage of market inefficiencies to generate superior returns. Empirical evidence indicates that this is not true.

There appears to be no credible study that documents the consistently superior performance of active managers in any major international market.[5] In fact, we believe the higher costs associated with international investing make it harder for the pros to beat foreign benchmarks than domestic benchmarks. Foreign markets are as well-developed and liquid as our own. Information in foreign markets moves quickly and prices adjust rapidly to new information, just as occurs here. Market efficiency is not limited to U.S. markets.

---

[5]Hawawini, G.A., "European Equity Markets: Price Behavior and Efficiency," a monograph of the Salomon Brothers Center for the Study of Financial Institutions (New York: New York University, 1984).

RECENT INTERNATIONAL STOCK RETURNS AND DIVERSIFICATION

International stock returns have lagged U.S. stock returns in the 1990s. International small-cap stocks have had lower returns than international large-cap stocks. This was particularly true in 1997 as international stocks, especially small-cap and emerging market stocks, significantly underperformed U.S. stocks. These results have caused many investors to question the wisdom of international diversification. Does international diversification still make sense? Let's answer this question first by examining the returns involved and then by reviewing what we are trying to accomplish when we diversify.

RECENT RETURNS

Table 7-3 and Figure 7-6 put the performance of international stocks into proper historical perspective. For the 29 years ending December 1997, the standard deviation of the differences between U.S. stock returns and international stock returns was 20.2 percent. Using historical standard deviation, we can calculate the range within which we would expect 95 percent of the differences between U.S. and foreign returns to fall. The size of the range declines with the square root of time.

The returns of international stocks have been disappointing in the late 1990s, but not unusual, and within the normal range of expectations. There have been large and frequent differences in the past between the returns of international stocks, measured by the EAFE index, and U.S. stocks, measured by the S&P 500 index. There have been as many disappointing periods for U.S. stocks as there have been for international stocks. Remarkably, the returns of the U.S. and foreign markets are within one percent of each other over the last 29 years.

TABLE 7-3

Average Annual Returns(%) Ending 12/97

Time Period	EAFE Index	S&P 500 Index	Difference	95% Confidence Limits (+/-)
1 Year	2.00	33.40	-31.40	39.60%
5 Years	11.70	20.20	-8.60	17.70%
10 Years	6.50	18.10	-11.50	12.60%
20 Years	14.40	16.70	-2.30	8.30%
28 Years	13.40	13.30	0.10	7.40%
40 Years				6.30%
50 Years				5.60%

Sources: Morgan Stanley Capital International, Standard & Poor's.

FIGURE 7-6

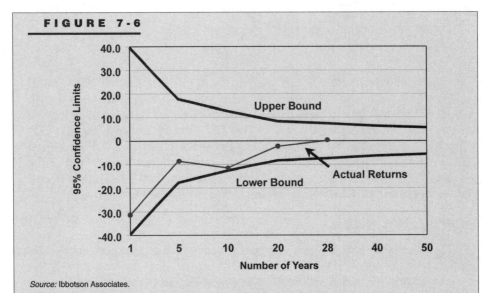

Source: Ibbotson Associates.

A COMPARISON OF TWO TIME PERIODS

Sometimes international markets do better than U.S. markets, and sometimes they do worse. For example, since 1986 there has been one period of high returns for international stocks, 1986-1990, and one period of low returns, 1991-1997. Table 7-4 shows the annualized compound returns for these two periods.

It is clear from the historical data that when U.S. stocks are weak, foreign stocks tend to be strong, and when foreign stocks are weak, U.S. stocks tend to be strong. These differences can last for a long time, and small-cap stocks tend to magnify this relationship since they tend to do best when their local market does well. This makes sense, because small companies typically have few exports and so are more closely tied to domestic markets.

Because international stocks tend to perform well when U.S. stocks do not, they are a good diversifier for U.S. investors. Furthermore, international small-cap stocks are even better for diversification than international large-cap stocks because they do best when foreign markets are strong.

WHY INVESTORS DIVERSIFY

Investors diversify in order to reduce risk. Because investment returns are not known before the fact, a rational investor diversifies by investing in multiple assets rather than betting the house on only one or two. To do this effectively, the assets must be sensitive to different risk factors so they will not tend to move together. Historical data, and clearly the results of recent years, indicate that foreign markets are sensitive to different risks than domestic markets are.

TABLE 7-4

U.S. Stocks	1/86-12/90	1/91-12/97
Large Cap (S&P 500 Index)	13.10%	19.87%
Small Cap (DFA US 9-10 Fund)	0.60%	23.25%
International Stocks	**1/86-12/90**	**1/91-12/97**
Large Cap (MSCI EAFE Index)	18.40%	8.07%
Small Cap (DFA Int'l Small Co. Fund)	28.30%	0.43%
	1/86-12/90 (Int'l Outperforms)	**1/91-12/97** (US Outperforms)
International Minus US		
Large Cap	5.30%	11.80%
Small Cap	27.70%	22.82%

Sources: Dimensional Fund Advisors, Morgan Stanley Capital International, Standard & Poor's.

It is easy to question international diversification after a period of foreign market underperformance. But remember, diversification never makes sense when viewed through the lenses of hindsight. Diversification is of no value with the benefit of hindsight because there is no risk when looking at past returns—even a chimpanzee could figure out where to invest after the fact. When looking backward, a rational investor does not choose diversification. He or she wants to concentrate investments in the best-performing asset class, which in the 1990s has been U.S. stocks.

In the real world, investors must make investment decisions without the benefit of hindsight. Diversification protects you from betting too heavily on what may turn out to be a loser. It is a form of insurance that helps you avoid unpredictable disaster. Knocking diversification after the fact is like wishing you hadn't bought fire insurance because your house did not burn down.

It would be nice if diversification always resulted in higher returns. It does not. Diversification is prudent, but it is not a free lunch. It has an economic cost equal to its economic benefit. In order to gain relative performance when U.S. stocks do poorly, you must be willing to lose relative performance when U.S. stocks do well. Diversification will always result in more consistent overall returns—never as good as the best-performing asset class, but never as bad as the worst-performing class.

Diversification is prudent investment policy. It should be followed during good times and bad because the future is always uncertain.

THE COSTS OF INVESTING OVERSEAS

Despite the evidence, international equity managers still argue that international markets are not efficient. Even if they are correct, the cost of capturing these inefficiencies would most likely negate their efforts. For example, Table 7-5 shows the estimated costs of a buy-side trade of $50,000 for each listed country. Trading costs include commissions, stamp duties, and custodial charges. They range from a high of 139 basis points in Singapore and Malaysia to a low of 38 basis points in the Netherlands. Given the already high fixed costs of international investing, high turnover rates for international portfolios can have a severe negative effect on returns.

TABLE 7-5

Estimated International Agency Costs (in basis points)

Country	Commissions	Stamp Duty	Custodial Transaction	Total Basis Points
Japan	65	0	7	72
Australia	75	30	17	122
Hong Kong	60	36	24	120
Singapore/Malaysia	100	15	24	139
United Kingdom	50	50	9	109
France	50	30	7	87
Germany	50	13	8	71
Italy	50	0	40	90
Switzerland	40	9	13	62
Netherlands	35	0	3	38
Belgium	90	20	15	125
Spain	70	0	5	75

Source: Dimensional Fund Advisors based on buy-side trades and an average estimated trade size of $50,000. As of June 30, 1993.

The significantly higher cost of investing overseas makes it even more important for you to be aware of the turnover ratio of the international mutual funds you use. An active manager trying to be competitive in Singapore with a 200 percent turnover rate would experience a 2.78 percent cost of doing business even without considering market impact costs. Combining these costs with the average expense ratio of international equity mutual funds of 1.80 percent results in a total cost to the investor of 4.58 percent.[6] We don't believe active management can overcome the effect of this expense on returns.

[6]This was calculated by screening the Morningstar OnDisc Database as of December 31, 1994 for all international equity funds that were deemed foreign and not institutional nor restricted-access funds. At that date there were 190 equity mutual funds that met this filter.

CURRENCY RISK WITH FOREIGN INVESTING

The dollar is flying, making sushi cheaper in Osaka, Hermes scarves more affordable in Paris, and a room in the Gritti Palace in Venice less of a strain on your wallet. But the greenback is also blowing big holes in many mutual funds that invest in European and Japanese securities.

Those were the opening lines of an April 17, 1997 *Wall Street Journal* article. The author, Michael Sesit, went on to note that while Fidelity's United Kingdom Fund was down 1.4 percent so far in 1997 when measured in U.S. dollars, the London Stock market was up 3 percent when measured in British pounds. And while shares in Tokyo were down 8 percent when measured in yen, some Japanese mutual funds were down as much as 26 percent when measured in U.S. dollars.

It is no wonder that investors are asking once again, "Shouldn't we hedge the currency risk of foreign stocks?" Anyone who suffers a dented fender on the way to the supermarket asks, "Did I really need that ice cream so badly that I had to get in the car and put my life and sanity in danger on the road?" It is natural to feel that way when we realize that our fenders would not have been dented had we stayed at home. It is natural to feel that way when we realize that our portfolios would not have been dented had we stayed in home currency. But is it wise never to venture away from home? Is it wise never to venture out of home currency?

The answer to the first question is obvious: The life of a hermit is not fun. The answer to the second question is not as obvious. American investors who buy Japanese stocks as part of their portfolios can choose one of two alternatives. One involves hedging the yen and the other does not. Both alternatives begin with a conversion of U.S. dollars to Japanese yen and using the yen to buy Japanese stocks.

In the first alternative, investors hedge exposure to the yen by selling (short) futures contracts on the yen. For example, on April 17, 1997, investors were able to sell a futures contract on the yen, expiring in September 1997, at 0.008114 dollars to the yen (123.24 yen to the dollar). The spot (cash) yen exchange rate on that day was different, 0.00793 dollars to the yen (126.05 yen to the dollar). The occurrence of a difference between the spot rate and the futures rate is the norm. It is called the forward premium when the futures rate exceeds the spot rate, and it is called the forward discount when the futures rate falls below the spot rate.

In our case of the yen on April 17, the futures rate (0.008114) exceeds the spot rate (0.00793), so we have a forward premium. Forward premiums or discounts are expressed in percentages reflecting the time period of the futures contract (in our case, from April to September). Hedging the exposure to the yen by selling futures on the yen is one alternative available to U.S. investors who hold Japanese stocks. The other alternative is simply holding Japanese stocks, and foregoing futures on the yen.

How would an investment in Japanese stocks have fared during January of 1997 for American investors who hedged by selling yen in the futures market? They would have lost 7.02 percent on Japanese stocks, measured in yen. The perspective of American investors is identical, so far, to the perspective of Japanese investors. But American investors would have gained 0.49 percent on the futures contracts. The total loss, measured in U.S. dollars, would have been 6.53 percent. American investors who held their Japanese stocks unhedged would have lost the same 7.02 percent on stocks, measured in yen. But they would have lost an additional 4.71 percent because the yen depreciated against the dollar. The total loss, measured in U.S. dollars, would have been 11.73 percent.

In hindsight, it surely would have been better to hedge the Japanese yen at the beginning of January 1997. But consider the situation in March of 1995, two years earlier. The return on Japanese stocks, measured in yen, was 2.95 percent. American investors who hedged the yen received an additional 0.34 percent forward premium. The total return, measured in U.S. dollars, was 3.29 percent. However, those who did not hedge the yen received much more. They received the same 2.95 percent return on Japanese stocks, measured in yen, but they also received an 11.08 percent return on the yen itself, since the value of the yen appreciated relative to the dollar. Their total return, measured in U.S. dollars, was 14.03 percent.

FIGURE 7-7

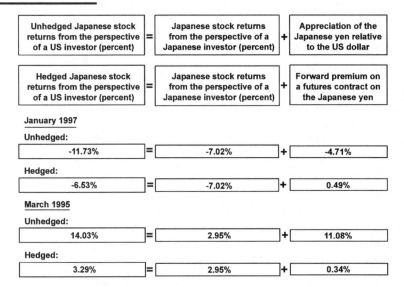

Source: Datastream database

TABLE 7-6

Hedged and Unhedged Portfolios

Year	Moderate Portfolio		Aggressive Portfolio	
	Unhedged	Hedged	Unhedged	Hedged
1980	19.75%	17.70%	23.08%	20.55%
1981	1.89%	8.09%	-0.10%	7.34%
1982	14.62%	19.67%	13.53%	19.70%
1983	18.03%	20.48%	20.40%	23.44%
1984	8.67%	15.23%	7.69%	15.66%
1985	36.15%	25.50%	41.69%	28.37%
1986	29.17%	21.58%	33.65%	24.22%
1987	10.71%	2.40%	11.59%	1.43%
1988	15.16%	18.22%	17.22%	21.01%
1989	19.41%	23.87%	21.08%	26.63%
1990	-6.70%	-10.36%	-10.14%	-14.41%
1991	17.20%	14.88%	18.36%	15.56%
1992	-1.21%	0.06%	-2.64%	-1.11%
1993	14.05%	12.08%	16.08%	13.66%
1994	4.16%	0.75%	5.09%	0.94%
1995	18.99%	20.15%	20.71%	22.14%
1996	9.86%	12.75%	10.94%	14.48%

	Geometric Mean Return	Arithmetic Mean Return	Standard Deviation of Return
Unhedged Moderate Portfolio	13.06%	13.52%	10.58%
Hedged Moderate Portfolio	12.69%	13.12%	9.87%
Unhedged Aggressive Portfolio	13.93%	14.60%	12.73%
Hedged Aggressive Portfolio	13.49%	14.09%	11.63%

Figure 7-7 shows that sometimes investors win by hedging foreign currencies and sometimes they lose. Do investors win more often than they lose? Consider returns on hedged and unhedged portfolios over the period from 1980 through 1996 (see Table 7-6). We simulate two portfolios, a moderate portfolio and an aggressive portfolio. The moderate portfolio is composed of 30 percent fixed-income securities (two-year Treasury notes) and 70 percent stocks (35 percent in the S&P 500, 17.5 percent in the Japanese Nikkei, 8.75 percent in the British FTSE, and 8.75 percent in the German DAX). The aggressive portfolio is composed of 15 percent fixed-income securities and 85 percent in stocks divided in proportions identical to those in the moderate portfolio. As you can see in Table 7-6, the hedged portfolios did better than the unhedged ones in 1995 and 1996. However, the unhedged portfolios performed better than the hedged ones in 1993 and 1994. Over the entire period, 1980 to 1996, the unhedged portfolios provided somewhat higher returns than the hedged ones. However, the unhedged portfolios also had somewhat higher standard deviations.

The analysis of returns and standard deviations indicates no clear advantage to either the hedged or unhedged portfolios, but other considerations give an advantage to the unhedged portfolios.

First, Modern Portfolio Theory has taught us to look at assets not in isolation but rather as part of an overall portfolio. An unhedged portfolio is a better choice for diversification reasons because it has a lower correlation than a hedged portfolio when combined with U.S. equities.

Second, the currency movements of different countries are not highly correlated. Some currencies go up against the dollar when others go down. This provides a diversification effect that reduces the overall foreign exchange risk of a widely diversified portfolio. Furthermore, the correlation between a stock market's movements and the changes in the value of its currency is usually close to zero.

Third, in the long run, exchange rates are primarily determined by inflation differentials between countries. Countries with high inflation rates see the value of their currencies decline relative to countries with low rates of inflation. Since stocks are claims on real assets and have fairly consistent real returns, hedging is unnecessary for a long-term investor. For example, a country with a high long-term inflation rate should have high enough local currency stock returns to offset the decline in the value of its currency and make it an attractive stock to hold even without a currency hedge.

Finally, the cost of hedging is high and hedging can be difficult to do. Hedging involves transaction costs, taxes, and administrative expenses that can be substantial, especially for a widely diversified portfolio with exposure to many different currencies. Futures contracts involve daily settlements, with cash paid or received depending on whether foreign currencies appreciated or depreciated that day. So hedging might involve daily cash outflows on futures while any counterpart gains on foreign stocks are unrealized. Of course, unrealized gains can always be realized, but realization of gains involves transaction costs and taxes.

After reviewing all factors, *we do not recommend hedging foreign currency risk* in your international equity portfolio.

A GLOBAL VILLAGE?

The world's economies are becoming more closely intertwined due to several factors, including:

1. the reduction in global trading barriers,
2. advancements in high technology,
3. the fall of Communism, and
4. increased wealth among developing countries.

We believe these developments are good for the U.S. economy and for global trade, but are they good for investors seeking the benefits of international diversification? Some people believe that increasing global economic ties between countries are causing the global stock markets to be more synchronized, hence reducing the value of international diversification.

While it is true that foreign markets do tend to move together during short-term times of distress, such as the Asian currency crisis of 1997, there is no trend toward increased correlation between markets over longer time periods. This is good news for investors because it means that the benefits of global diversification remain intact.

Figure 7-8 shows the correlation between the S&P 500 and EAFE from 1970 to 1997, using ten-year rolling time periods. As you can see, the correlation between U.S. and foreign markets is lower in the 1990s than it was in the 1970s.

Why should this be so? The answer is that although the world's economies are getting more closely connected due to reducing global trade barriers and rapidly improving communication and information technology, their rates of productivity and economic growth, as well as fiscal and monetary policies, remain independent. Furthermore, we would expect that an increase in global trade would lead to increasing economic specialization as countries focus more intently on those areas in which they have a comparative advantage (e.g., the U.S. makes computers and movies, while Japan makes cars, VCRs, and CD players). All of these reasons suggest that relatively uncorrelated global economic cycles and a low correlation between national stock markets will continue.

FIGURE 7-8

Correlation Between S&P 500 and EAFE

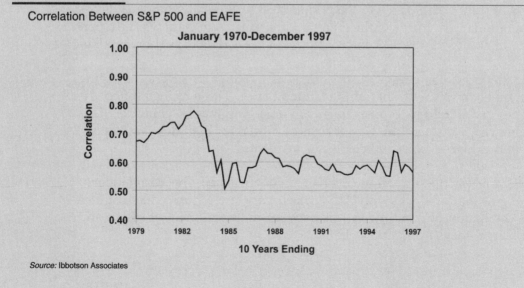

Source: Ibbotson Associates

EMERGING MARKETS

Many institutional investors now recognize emerging markets as a separate and distinct asset class. Although emerging markets make up only about 13 percent of the world's stock market capitalization, we believe they constitute an important asset class for a global portfolio. The term *emerging markets* refers to the stock markets of the world's developing countries whose economies are growing fast enough to deserve to be called emerging. Emerging countries experience rapid growth and improvements in their political, social, and economic conditions. You might conclude that the higher rates of economic growth in these countries should lead to higher stock returns. This is a common message communicated by the financial press and investment professionals.

While it is true that emerging market countries have higher economic growth rates than the developed world, that fact alone does not mean their stock returns will be higher. Why not? Because this information is widely known and stock prices already reflect the market's expectations of high growth.

We too believe that long-term stock returns in emerging markets will be higher than in the developed world. However, higher expected returns are not due to faster economic growth. *Higher returns represent a reward for accepting higher risk.* Emerging market investing involves substantial risks including political instability, extreme market volatility, lack of liquidity, dramatic currency devaluation, high transaction costs, and regulatory risk. A lack of reliable information is also an issue because many of emerging market countries have low accounting standards and very poor financial disclosure. These risks are much greater than those in developed countries, but they are well known and researched by the market.

One example of the higher risk of emerging markets is the extreme level of price volatility. Over the period 1988 to 1996, the standard deviation of monthly returns of the emerging markets asset class was 6.16 percent, almost twice the 3.33 percent figure of the S&P 500, as shown in Figure 7-9.

Table 7-7 compares the sovereign debt ratings of several emerging market countries with that of the United States. These ratings reflect the higher perceived risk of investments in emerging market countries. This higher risk translates into higher costs of capital for both debt and equity, as well as higher expected returns for investors.

In addition to higher expected returns, emerging market stocks will give your portfolio another layer of diversification. The correlation of emerging market stocks with U.S. stocks is very low. Figure 7-10 illustrates the correlation of monthly returns between emerging market stocks and U.S. large stocks from 1988 to 1996.

FIGURE 7-9

Monthly Returns of Emerging Market Stocks and U.S. Large Stocks 1988–1996

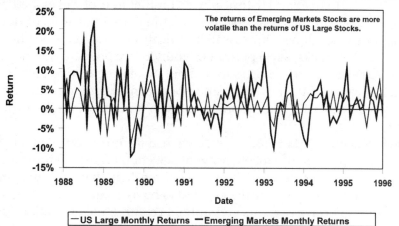

Source: Ibbotson Associates, Morgan Stanley Capital International

TABLE 7-7

Sovereign Ratings

Country	Foreign Currency (LT)	
	Moody's	S&P
Argentina	B1	BB-
Brazil	B1	B+
Chile	Baa1	A-
Israel	A3	A-
Malaysia	A1	BB
Mexico	Ba2	BB+
Philippines	Ba2	AA-
South Korea	A1	A
Thailand	A2	B
Turkey	B1/B2	B
United States	Aaa	AAA

Source: Moody's Corporate Credit Reports, S&P's Sovereign Reports, August 1997

In addition to emerging markets stocks having a low correlation with the U.S. market, the correlations among the individual emerging markets themselves are low. As you know from Modern Portfolio Theory, the lower the correlation an asset has with the rest of your portfolio, the more useful it is as a diversifier. Historically, a combination of developed and emerging market equities has been less volatile than a portfolio of developed market stocks alone. Our research indicates that a small position in emerging market stocks, say 5 percent of your equity portion, can increase the expected return of your portfolio without increasing its overall volatility. In fact, because of the low correlation between emerging markets and other asset classes, the allocation may even reduce overall portfolio volatility.

The emerging market asset classes we use for our clients contain securities from countries that meet stringent selection criteria. For example, selected countries must have well-organized markets that provide ample liquidity to their shares. Countries must also have a developed legal system that protects property rights and upholds contractual obligations. It is also important to keep in mind that while these markets may be defined as emerging, the companies whose stocks are being purchased are well-established in those countries. Typical holdings are national banks, land developers, and phone companies of various countries. Our current country selections include Indonesia, Turkey, Argentina, Malaysia, the Philippines, Portugal, Israel, Mexico, Brazil, Thailand, South Korea, and Chile.

FIGURE 7·10

Monthly Returns of Emerging Markets Stocks and U.S. Large Stocks, 1988–1996

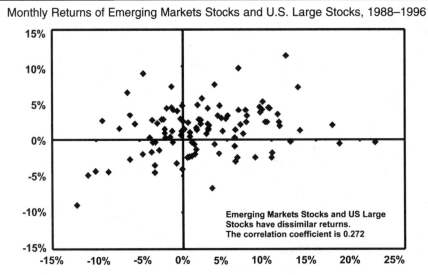

Emerging Markets Stocks and US Large Stocks have dissimilar returns. The correlation coefficient is 0.272

Sources: Ibbotson Associates, Morgan Stanley Capital International

CHAPTER

Tax-Efficient Investing

*M*ost retail mutual funds are inherently not very tax efficient as investment vehicles; their after-tax returns are far lower than their pre-tax returns. According to Morningstar, for the ten-year period ending June 30, 1996, the average growth mutual fund returned 12.0 percent per year pre-tax, but only 9.4 percent after-tax (assuming maximum brackets). This reduction in return is due to dividend and capital gain distributions made by the funds, which are taxable to investors. From a tax perspective, the ideal mutual fund would make no taxable distributions whatever; its pre-tax and after-tax returns would be identical. Such a perfectly tax-efficient fund is not practical, but some funds are better than others at deferring taxes and improving their after-tax returns.

Let's compare three hypothetical mutual funds: a traditional tax-inefficient fund, a capital gain tax-efficient fund, and a totally tax-efficient fund. Each fund has a dividend yield of 2 percent and capital appreciation of 8 percent, for an average annual return of 10 percent. In this example, we assume that ordinary income is taxed at 39.6 percent and capital gains at 20 percent. No state income tax is assumed.

> **Fund 1: The traditional tax-inefficient fund.** The traditional tax-inefficient fund distributes all its ordinary dividend income each year, and also realizes and distributes a significant portion of its capital gains on average. We call this the tax-inefficient fund, but it is really the traditional mutual fund. Because most retail funds have relatively high turnover rates—currently averaging about 80 percent per year—they are forced to distribute much of their annual capital appreciation. To keep our example simple, we assume a capital gain distribution rate of 100 percent.

Fund 2: The capital gain tax-efficient fund. The second fund is the capital gain tax-efficient fund. In this fund, all dividend and interest income is distributed annually and is taxable. However, the fund is able to avoid realizing capital gains, so no capital gain distributions are ever made.

Fund 3: The totally tax-efficient fund. The totally tax-efficient fund makes no taxable distributions whatever. It is able to avoid not only capital gain distributions, but also ordinary income distributions.

In Figure 8-1 we compare the returns on each type of fund on an after-tax basis. The differences are significant and can represent substantial dollars when compounded over the lifetime of an investor.

TAX-EFFICIENT INVESTMENT STRATEGIES

We believe that passive strategies—asset class investing and pure indexing—are the most tax-efficient strategies available. The largest and oldest mutual fund utilizing a pure indexing strategy is the Vanguard Index 500, which tracks the performance of the S&P 500 index. Since its inception in September 1976, the fund's annual compound rate of return has been 14.2 percent. However, the only investor who actually received this return was one who had paid no taxes along the way. Without paying taxes, a $1,000 investment in this fund at inception would have grown to $14,882.

FIGURE 8-1

Hypothetical Funds. Compound Rates of Return After Taxes on Distributions

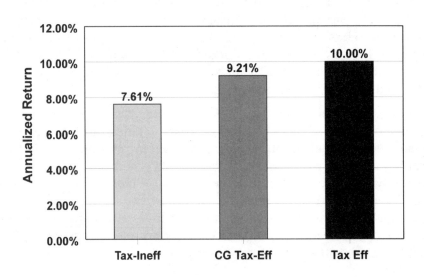

FIGURE 8-2

Vanguard Index 500 Growth of $1,000 After Taxes on Distributions

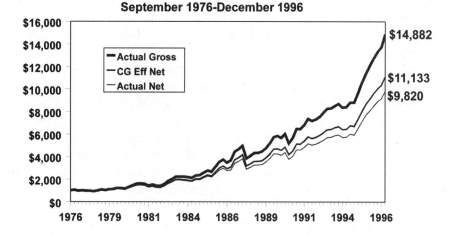

September 1976-December 1996

Unfortunately, unless you are a tax-exempt investor you must pay taxes on dividend and capital gain distributions. This reduces your realized return. Given our tax rate assumptions, a $1,000 investment would have grown to only $9,820 after-tax. This lowers the rate of return to 11.9 percent, which is a significant erosion of capital for one of the most tax-efficient mutual funds available today (see Figure 8-2).

We could help ourselves if we could implement a more tax-efficient strategy. But how would we go about doing it? First of all, we would want to hold onto all of our winning stocks. By not selling them, we would not realize any capital gains. If we did have to sell stock for a gain, we would also sell enough losers to create an equally offsetting loss.

We would then have to somehow offset ordinary income distributions. One way of doing this is to create deductible expenses by borrowing against the securities in the portfolio and using the interest paid to offset ordinary income. Unfortunately, with an S&P 500 Index Fund, for example, you would need about 50 percent leverage to shelter all of the income. An alternative would be to buy and hold stocks with low dividend yields, but that would put our portfolio in lower expected return growth stocks.

Today there are a number of tax-managed mutual funds being marketed aggressively. These funds attempt to be capital gain tax-efficient. None of them is trying to be *totally* tax-efficient. The longest-running fund of this type that we know of is the Schwab 1000 Fund managed by Charles

Schwab investment management. This fund has been able to avoid capital gain distributions since its inception in April 1991, but it has made income distributions.

Why aren't we seeing more of these capital gain tax-efficient funds? One reason is that when a fund minimizes capital gain distributions it creates a substantial deferred capital gain problem, because techniques used to defer capital gains in the near term are likely to result in huge capital gain distributions sometime later. By using a strategy of deferring capital gain distributions, the fund creates a large and growing inventory of low-cost basis stocks. This is a huge potential tax liability for shareholders, and there is the potential for a meltdown.

If the mutual fund suffers from net redemptions—perhaps due to fickle investors selling after a period of poor performance—it will be forced to realize some of its built-up gains. The resulting taxable distributions could be very large and would certainly be an unpleasant surprise to the fund's long-term, loyal shareholders.

Table 8-1 indicates that potential capital gains exposure—defined as capital appreciation as a percentage of a mutual fund's total assets—is growing substantially for many funds. One particular fund, Stagecoach Equity Index, began operation in January 1984 and now has a 60 percent potential capital gain exposure. In other words, 60 percent of the fund's assets consist of built-up capital appreciation. If the fund manager were forced to sell these profitable holdings, the sale would result in a significant capital gain for shareholders. There is no reason a taxable investor would want to buy this fund, given all the other choices available.

TABLE 8-1

Selected Mutual Funds through December 1997

Tax Managed Funds	Inception Date	Fund PCGE
Schwab 1000	Apr-91	38%
Vanguard Tax-Mgd Cap Apprec	Sep-94	30%
Vanguard Tax-Mgd Grth & Inc	Sep-94	25%
Index Funds		
DFA U.S. Large Company	Dec-90	33%
Fidelity Spartan US Equity Index	Feb-88	35%
SEI Index S&P 500 Index A	Aug-85	9%
Stagecoach Equity Index A	Jan-84	60%
Vanguard Index 500	Aug-76	36%

FIGURE 8-3

Tax Efficiency and Investment Strategy

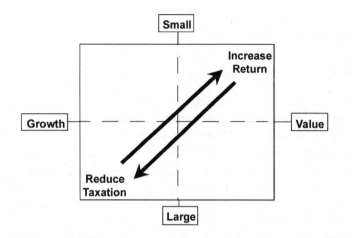

There are problems in building a totally tax-efficient fund. Minimizing income distributions is only accomplished by increasing risk through the use of leverage, or by lowering expected returns through investing in low-yielding growth stocks. These strategies would give our fund undesirable characteristics that are detrimental to our overall investment strategy.

It is important to recognize that there is a trade-off between tax efficiency and investing for higher returns, as shown in Figure 8-3. This represents a dilemma for all taxable investors. *Investment strategies that invest in higher expected return asset categories are typically not the most tax-efficient strategies.*

Consider small-cap stocks, for example. They have higher expected returns than large-cap stocks, but a focused small-cap stock portfolio strategy is relatively tax inefficient. This is because you have to sell your winners as they get larger and grow out of the portfolio in order to stay invested in small-cap stocks. This profit taking causes you to realize capital gains, which are taxable. In contrast, large-cap stock strategies are more tax efficient. For example, with a large-cap strategy you sell losing stocks as their market capitalization and stock prices decline until they drop out of the portfolio. Selling the losers involves less taxable gain than selling winners; it is more tax efficient.

Maintaining a portfolio of value stocks that have higher expected returns than growth stocks also results in tax inefficiencies. Most value strategies buy stocks that have low market prices relative to various measures of underlying value. Capturing the returns of this asset class involves selling the stocks that have increased the most in price, which moves them out of the value asset class. A growth strategy, on the other hand, involves investing in a lower expected return asset class, but is more tax efficient because growth strategies involve selling stocks that have declined in price and moved out of the growth asset class. Because these stocks have declined in price, selling them creates a smaller capital gain or perhaps even a loss.

FOCUS ON ECONOMIC VALUE, NOT TAX DEFERRAL

You can probably remember a time when you lost money because of your desire to avoid taxes. This happened to many investors in the 1980s who invested in tax-oriented real estate partnerships and other deals that lacked economic value. As author Charles Ellis said in his book, *Investment Policy,* "Never do anything for tax reasons." We suggest you focus on economics and sound investment policy, rather than on tax deferral. Once you satisfy those requirements, you can then arrange your assets to maximize after-tax returns.

What are the practical implications of this advice? First of all, we believe the extra returns available through higher-risk asset classes—even though less tax efficient—are large enough to make them worth pursuing. You should invest in value stocks and small stocks.

In addition, we suggest that you segregate your funds to optimize after-tax returns. For example, fixed income securities should be held in tax-exempt accounts. Large company stocks and value stocks are also best held in tax-exempt accounts. Small company and emerging market stocks are good choices for taxable accounts. The best way for you to divide your portfolio will depend, of course, on your own personal financial and tax situation. A qualified advisor can help you determine the optimal way to arrange your asset classes.

TAX-FREE SECURITIES AS AN ASSET CLASS

All things equal, investors would prefer to have tax-free income rather than taxable income, because investors feel that taxes are amounts the government takes from them, rather than amounts earned for services provided. We often hear our clients say, "I don't want Uncle Sam to take my money." Unfortunately, many investors take their desire to avoid taxes too far—often to the point of reducing their after-tax return just to avoid the tax. We think this is the case with most investors who own municipal bonds. In reality, they would be better off with U.S. government or high-quality corporate securities.

In the short-maturity marketplace, municipal bonds are priced with tax-equivalent yields about the same as government and high-quality corporate bonds, even for high tax bracket investors. Viewed from the point of view of yield alone, short-term municipal bonds seem at least worthy of consideration. However, there are two important drawbacks to municipal bonds that cause us to recommend that most investors avoid them. First, they often have call provisions that allow issuing agencies to redeem the bonds before maturity. When interest rates go down, for example, the issuer may call or redeem the bonds. Although this helps keep the issuer's financing costs in check, it reduces investors' upside price potential and forces them to reinvest principal when rates are low.

More importantly, municipal bonds have high trading costs because there are large bid-ask spreads and significant market impact costs in the municipal marketplace. These additional costs eliminate the benefits of using an enhanced trading strategy such as the matrix pricing strategy we use in our government and corporate bond portfolios. The turnover required would simply be too costly. Because of their high trading costs, municipal bonds are only suitable for buy-and-hold investors who want to hold longer-maturity bonds or high-yield municipals.

For these reasons we believe most investors are better off with taxable securities rather than municipal bonds. While paying taxes is not pleasant, it's better to pay the tax if one can get higher after-tax returns by doing so.

In your tax-deferred accounts we recommend that you use short-term, high-quality corporate bonds. In your taxable accounts we suggest short-term U.S. government bonds if you are subject to state income tax (since interest from U.S. government obligations is not subject to state income tax) and short-term, high-quality corporate bonds if you are not.

9

How to Build the Optimal Portfolio

We now have seven asset class building blocks: cash equivalents, two-year fixed income, U.S. large company stocks, U.S. small company stocks, international large company stocks, international small company stocks, and emerging market stocks. How do you determine the optimal combination of these asset classes for your portfolio?

FIVE STEPS IN ALLOCATING YOUR PORTFOLIO AMONG EACH ASSET CLASS

Step 1. Determine the expected rate of return of each asset class. Before you invest in any asset, you should have an estimate of its expected returns. You want to know that the expected rate of return justifies its inclusion in your portfolio. The expected return is a target rate of return against which you can measure realized performance. Higher risk asset classes will have higher expected returns and lower risk asset classes will have lower expected returns.

Step 2. Know the risk level of the asset class. Risk is the uncertainty of future rates of return. You can measure the historical risk of an investment by reviewing the standard deviation of its past returns. Securities within the asset class are priced to reflect their perceived risk by the market.

Step 3. Calculate the correlation coefficients of all the asset classes. Correlation coefficients measure the dissimilar price movements among asset classes by quantifying the degree to which they move together. Values range from +1.000 to –1.000. A correlation coefficient of +1.000 implies that the returns of the assets move in lockstep with each other, although not necessarily by equal increments. A coefficient of –1.000 means they move in opposite directions at the same time.

The use of low or negative correlation is a powerful tool in providing effective diversification. Many asset classes have historically shown a pattern of moving dissimilarly in time, degree, or direction. Combining asset classes with low correlations is a proven tool for reducing the volatility of a portfolio.

Step 4. Solve for the optimal combination of asset classes for each level of risk. Once expected returns, standard deviations, and correlation coefficients have been determined, optimal portfolios can be created. Optimal portfolios lie within a range of efficient portfolios called the efficient frontier. The efficient frontier consists of portfolios with the highest expected rate of return for each given level of risk. Prudent investors restrict their choices of portfolios to those within the efficient frontier representing their unique risk tolerance level.

Step 5. Identify your risk tolerance. Many financial advisors have developed questionnaires to quantify the risk level investors are willing to take. Typically, these questionnaires incorporate different qualitative measures of risk. We have found them to be too subjective. Your answers are influenced significantly by how you feel on the day you complete the questionnaire. We prefer a quantitative approach; it's much more effective and reliable.

The approach we use is to determine how your portfolio would have performed in very bad times, such as from January 1973 through December 1974. For example, assume that the asset class portfolio you are considering lost 30 percent of its value during the 1973–1974 period. If you had $200,000 invested, your portfolio would have decreased in value to $140,000. Would you have closed your account and fired your financial advisor? Probably, if you didn't understand the risks ahead of time.

You are in control if you predetermine the risk level that you are willing to accept before you invest. Over the long term, more risk will result in higher rates of return, but only if you stay with the strategy. We will return to this concept in Chapter Ten when we discuss building your investment policy statement.

DOING THE CALCULATIONS

The mathematical calculations necessary to determine the range of efficient portfolios are included in the Appendix. Mathematical formulas can sidetrack many investors and can sometimes seem overwhelming and complicated. If you are working with an advisor you do not need to know how to calculate each of the five steps, but working through them will help you understand the end result.

Expected Rates of Return

In calculating the expected rates of return for each asset class you must recognize that these are theoretical returns. The expected rate of return is the forecasted return based on the historical arithmetic average returns for each asset class. If you are going to invest in a portfolio that includes equities, your minimum time horizon should be at least five years, but preferably ten years or more. You should recalculate expected returns at least annually.

Expected Risk

In Table 9-1, we illustrate expected standard deviations for each asset class. You can calculate these for yourself using a spreadsheet program if you have the historical return data for the asset classes you are considering.

TABLE 9-1

Expected Standard Deviations

Asset Class	Annualized Standard Deviation
Money Market	3.3%
Two-Year US Government	3.9%
US Large Company Stocks	20.3%
US Small Company Stocks	38.5%
Int'l Large Stocks	20.3%
Int'l Small Stocks	38.5%
Emerging Market Stocks	29.0%

TABLE 9-2

Asset Class Correlation Coefficients 1972–1997

	Money Market	One Year	US Large	US Small	Int'l Large	Int'l Small	Emerging Markets
Money Market	1.000						
Two-Year US Government	0.571	1.000					
US Large Company Stocks	-0.095	0.184	1.000				
US Small Company Stocks	-0.116	0.026	0.835	1.000			
Int'l Large Stocks	-0.154	0.101	0.576	0.538	1.000		
Int'l Small Stocks	-0.172	-0.027	0.431	0.508	0.849	1.000	
Emerging Market Stocks	-0.167	-0.001	0.491	0.547	0.706	0.746	1.000

Correlation Coefficients

One of the most important components of investing is understanding the idea of correlation. Common sense dictates that we don't put all our eggs in one basket. More scientifically, by combining assets with low correlations, we can lower overall portfolio risk while enhancing risk-adjusted rates of return. We recommend using the longest time period of data available when analyzing the correlation coefficients of the asset classes.

Table 9-2 illustrates the correlation coefficients for each of our asset classes from 1972 through 1997.

Now that we've calculated the expected rates of return, standard deviations, and correlation coefficients for each of our asset classes, we have to determine the optimal combination of asset classes that results in the highest rate of return for each level of risk. These portfolios lie within a range of efficient portfolios called the efficient frontier. The efficient frontier is a continuum of efficient portfolios. Rational and prudent investors restrict their choice of a portfolio to one that lies within the efficient frontier and represents their own risk tolerance level.

In Figure 9-1, we illustrate the efficient frontier for our five model portfolios. We call them Global Defensive, Global Conservative, Global Moderate, Global Aggressive, and Global Equity. Their equity allocations are 25 percent, 50 percent, 70 percent, 85 percent, and 98 percent, respectively. Once you determine your risk tolerance, you can select the model portfolio that suits you.

Don't be swayed by the names of the portfolios. Each investor has his or her own risk tolerance. What is right for you may not be right for someone else, even someone who has similar objectives and constraints.

Generally, we find that younger people have a higher tolerance for risk than older investors. Younger people may feel that they have both the time and earning capability to recover from a big loss, while older investors may feel they do not have this luxury. However, as older investors become more sophisticated and gain an understanding of asset class investing, they often are more comfortable with risk because they understand and expect some short-term market volatility. They understand that some volatility is necessary to have the potential for higher returns in the long run.

FIGURE 9-1

The Efficient Frontier

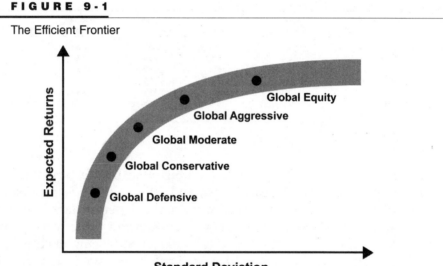

To evaluate your tolerance for risk, we suggest that you consider the historical performance of different portfolios, especially during declining markets. This is most easily done by constructing asset class portfolios using historical data and simulating how they would have performed in both up and down markets. You can then select a portfolio with which you feel comfortable.

One of the benefits of asset class investing is that you can invest in the exact asset classes you use in your historical research. This allows you to reliably estimate the degree of risk inherent in your portfolio. Traditional actively managed funds, on the other hand, rarely resemble any definitive asset class. Their asset mix changes often and is usually composed of securities of several different asset categories. This makes it virtually impossible to create a portfolio of actively managed funds that has the characteristics of your historical model portfolio.

In Table 9-3, we list the asset class composition of our five model portfolios.

TABLE 9-3

Asset Class Composition

	Global Defensive	Global Conservative	Global Moderate	Global Aggressive	Global Equity
Money Market	5%	5%	5%	5%	2%
Two Year Fixed Corp.	70%	45%	25%	10%	0%
US Large Company Stocks	9%	18%	25%	30%	34%
US Small Company Stocks	4%	7%	10%	13%	15%
Int'l Large Company Stocks	8%	16%	22%	27%	31%
Int'l Small Company Stocks	3%	6%	9%	11%	13%
Emerging Market Stocks	1%	3%	4%	4%	5%

In Figures 9-2 through 9-6, we have illustrated the performance of our model portfolios over 1-year, 5-year, and 10-year periods. To determine your own risk tolerance, look at the annual performance of the model portfolios in their worst year. For all the portfolios the worst year is 1974. Would you have stayed invested after experiencing such a decline? If your answer is no, then reduce your risk by considering a model portfolio with less equity exposure. If your answer is yes, then consider moving up in risk to a higher equity exposure portfolio.

Notice the five-year performance numbers. From 1972 to 1997, there is never a five-year period during which the model portfolios do not have a positive return despite some poor results from some of the individual asset classes. Effective diversification has reduced risk. This is the way asset class investing works. It allows you to ride through business cycles with peace of mind, knowing that free markets are working for you in the long run.

FIGURE 9-2

Global Defensive Portfolio

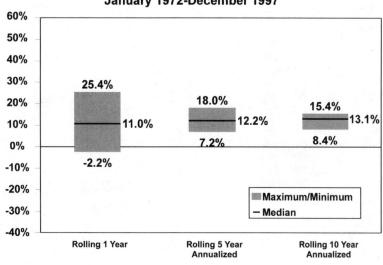

January 1972-December 1997

FIGURE 9-3

Global Conservative Portfolio

January 1972-December 1997

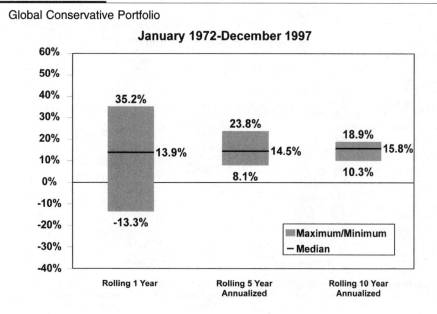

Global Moderate Portfolio

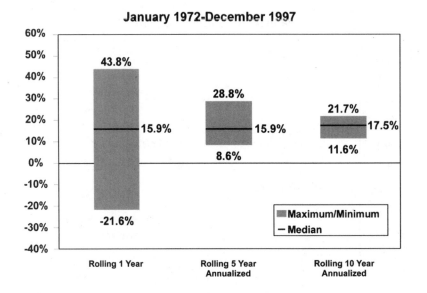

January 1972-December 1997

F I G U R E 9 - 5

Global Aggressive Portfolio

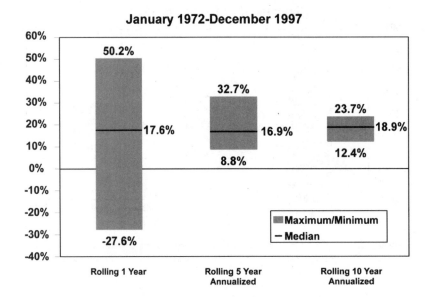

January 1972-December 1997

FIGURE 9-6

Global Equity Portfolio

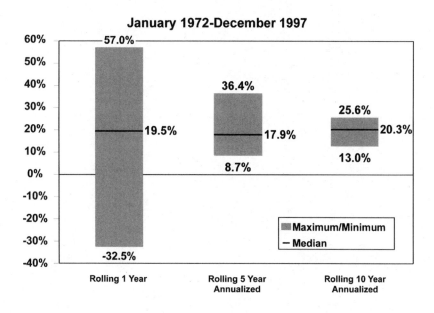

Your Investment Policy Statement

One of the most powerful tools to increase the probability of your success is an investment policy statement. In this chapter, you will learn how to put your own personal investment program into a written, workable strategy that you can implement in both good and bad markets. You might compare this to a business plan; very few businesses succeed without one. Institutional investors call these written investment plans "investment policy statements." We feel it is the critical first step to successful investing. We prepare one for each of our clients, without exception.

An investment policy statement defines an investor's objectives and constraints, including risk tolerance, return objectives, time horizon, liquidity needs, the amount of funds available for investment, and the investment methodology to be followed. A written investment policy statement enables you to clearly communicate your long-term goals and objectives to your advisor, or it serves as a personal guideline if you are implementing your investment strategy on your own. The written policy statement helps you maintain a sound long-term plan, even when short-term market movements are causing you to second-guess yourself.

We believe all investors should have an investment policy statement that outlines their goals and how their money will be invested to reach those goals. Investors can get caught up in the emotions of the day. It's only through discipline and long-term planning that they are going to be successful and not fall back into old habits. In the heat of a market downturn, it is critical to have a well-thought-out strategy so you don't make emotional errors.

Creating an investment policy statement embodies the essence of the financial planning process. It includes: (1) assessing where you are now, (2) determining where you want to go, and (3) developing a strategy to get there. Having a policy statement compels you to be a more disciplined investor, which increases the probability that you will reach your investment goals. If you are a trustee, a written investment policy statement will go a long way toward insuring that you meet your fiduciary responsibilities.

EIGHT STEPS TO ESTABLISHING AN INVESTMENT POLICY

Step 1. Set your long-term goals and objectives clearly and concisely. Long-term goals can be anything from early retirement to purchasing a new home. One of the most common goals our clients have is financial independence. What that means to our clients is that their investment portfolio can provide them with the income necessary to maintain their quality of life without worrying about the future. This is just as important for clients who are still working as for those who are already retired. Be sure to quantify your goals and rank them in order of importance to you.

Step 2. Define the level of risk you are willing to accept. Along the road to reaching your financial goals there are going to be bumps caused by downturns in various markets. It is important for you to decide the amount of risk you're willing to tolerate. In designing your portfolio you should determine the approximate loss you're willing to accept without terminating your investment program. Since no one can predict market movements, you have to be able to weather any storm and stay invested throughout your time horizon.

The best way to determine the level of risk in a portfolio is to look at its performance in bad markets, such as 1973 and 1974. In those two years the Standard & Poor's 500 Index lost 37.2 percent of its value and U.S. small company stocks lost 56.5 percent. Statistically, there is about a 5 percent chance of experiencing a similar downturn in any given year. You must create a balanced portfolio and have the discipline that will enable you stay invested through such a heart-wrenching bear market.

Step 3. Establish the expected time horizon for your investment. Each investor has to determine the investment period for his or her capital. We consider five years to be the minimum acceptable time commitment for any portfolio containing equity securities, but we prefer to see horizons of ten years or more. This is usually not a problem, because an individual's time horizon is usually equal to life expectancy. For example, the joint life expectancy of a 65-year-old couple is 25 years, and for a 75-year-old couple, 16 years, according to IRS tables. Any portfolio with a shorter time horizon should be comprised predominantly of fixed-income securities.

Time commitment is critical. The investment process should be viewed as a long-term plan for achieving desired results. One-year volatility can be significant, but over longer periods the range of returns is greatly reduced, as shown in Figure 10-1.

Step 4. Determine the rate of return objective. All investors have a rate of return they need to achieve their financial goals. You want to make sure that the portfolio you select has an expected return that is high enough to satisfy your particular return requirements. In getting started, you should write down a range of returns that would be acceptable. Remember, your portfolio's expected return is a direct result of your willingness to take prudent risk. Table 10-1 shows the return profiles of each of our model portfolios. You can use these ranges of returns as a framework to determine the expected return for your portfolio as well as its component asset classes.

FIGURE 10-1

S&P 500 Return Distribution

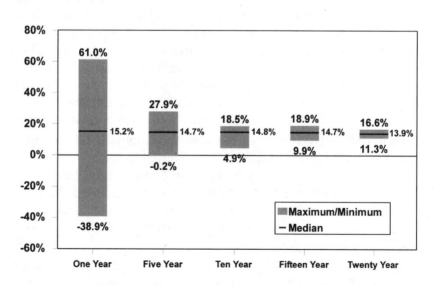

Model Portfolio Expected Returns

Asset Class	Expected Returns
Cash Equivalents	5.1%
Two-Year US Corporate	7.1%
US Large Company Stocks	13.5%
US Small Company Stocks	19.4%
Int'l Large Company Stocks	13.5%
Int'l Small Company Stocks	19.4%
Emerging Market Stocks	16.5%

Model	Expected Returns
Global Defensive	9.0%
Global Conservative	11.1%
Global Moderate	12.7%
Global Aggressive	14.0%
Global Equity	15.1%

We encourage you to focus on the historical returns of your portfolio and its asset classes over long periods. Don't just look at the recent past; it's not likely to be repeated. You also want to examine some difficult periods, such as the 1973–1974 bear market, to see if you could have stayed the course.

Step 5. Select the asset classes to be used to build your portfolio. In Chapter 6 we examined the institutional and retail asset class mutual funds available to you. Get out a sheet of paper and list all the asset classes and corresponding funds you want to consider for your portfolio. You may be surprised to find differences between the funds you've been using in the past and those you should be using. Remember that you want funds with low expenses, low turnover rates, low trading costs, and consistent asset allocation.

Step 6. Document the investment methodology to be used in managing your portfolio. We see no benefit in using actively managed funds that engage in subjective forecasting, stock selection, or market timing activities. You should avoid those funds in favor of passively managed asset class funds. Both financial theory and empirical evidence support the superiority of asset class funds over conventional funds.

Step 7. Establish a strategic implementation plan. Once you've identified the first six components of your investment policy you need to determine how you're going to allocate your capital to each asset class. Previously, we illustrated the mathematical techniques you can use to determine your optimal portfolio. An easier way is simply to use one of our model portfolios.

Step 8. Establish the means for making periodic adjustments to your portfolio. The investment policy statement creates a benchmark against which you can measure investment portfolio performance. If your goals and objectives have been clearly defined it becomes much easier to determine how the portfolio is performing relative to these goals and objectives.

To be a successful investor, you must take full responsibility for your investment portfolio decisions. Being responsible, however, does not mean that you need to become a bona fide expert in portfolio theory and make all the difficult asset allocation decisions yourself. Instead, you can familiarize yourself with the operating rules contained in this book and decide whether you want to manage your portfolio on your own or seek a competent investment adviser to assist you. Either way, the written investment policy statement will enable you to better define your investment expectations. It will also put you in a position to decide how to best implement your asset class portfolio.

PRUDENT INVESTOR GUIDELINES

Most individual investors are not trustees who are subject to the following guidelines. However, if you are a trustee it is important that you understand your responsibilities and how asset class investing can help you fulfill your fiduciary obligations.

The written investment policy statement creates a road map for plan fiduciaries to meet the legal requirements of the prudent investor rules. The written plan also provides standards against which the trustee can be judged. The investment policy statement must be clear and specific enough to be a working document. Broad-based generalities will not serve as investment objectives. Being specific is the key to providing a proper, working investment plan.

The American Law Institute *Restatement of the Law Third,* Prudent Investor Rules, instructs trustees and courts that:

- Sound diversification is fundamental to risk management and is therefore ordinarily required of trustees.
- Risk and returns are so directly related that trustees have a duty to analyze and make conscious decisions concerning the level of

risk appropriate to the purposes, requirements, and circumstances of the trust.

- Trustees have a duty to avoid fees, transaction costs, and other expenses that are not justified by needs and realistic objectives of the trust's investment program.
- The fiduciary duty of impartiality requires a balancing of elements of return between current income and the protection of purchasing power.
- Trustees may have the duty as well as the authority to delegate as prudent investors would.

The prudent investor rules have become laws in many states. We feel that it is critical to follow these guidelines and prepare an investment policy statement that will protect you and your family.

STAYING ON TRACK—THE SOURCE OF WINNING RESULTS

With all the distractions you face, it is easy to get sidetracked. With stockbrokers calling you with their latest, hottest investment product; investment magazine headlines promising overnight investment success; and television experts pitching their investment secrets, there will be times when you will second-guess your new investment strategy, asset class investing.

When one asset class is performing at record pace the naysayers will try to play to your emotions and advise you to put your money in the hot market. You must not give in to their persuasive sales pitches. Maintaining the discipline of your investment policy and having faith in the long-term wealth-building capability of the capital markets is crucial for success.

While keeping your eye on the long-term, you must have reasonable expectations for the short-term. Reviewing the last 72 years of stock market performance will help you better understand what you might expect. During the period from January 1926 through December 1997, an investor would have had to earn a 3.1 percent average return per year just to keep pace with inflation. On average, it takes $9.05 today to buy the same goods that $1 bought in 1926. All investors want, at a minimum, to maintain their purchasing power.

Stock market investing has maintained purchasing power very effectively over the long term. The Standard & Poor's 500 index has grown at an average rate of 11.0 percent per year from January 1926 to December 1997. One dollar invested in stocks comprising the S&P 500 would have grown to $1,829 over this period. Even after considering income taxes and the spending of dividend income, common stocks still kept pace with inflation. Higher expected returns are the reason that we invest in equities.

Stock returns include a risk premium over Treasury bills to compensate investors for the additional risk of investing in the stock market. However, this risk premium is not constant each month or quarter. For example, by removing the best performing month of each calendar year for Standard & Poor's 500, we find that average returns drop from 11.0 percent per year to a meager 1.97 percent. On average, *over 90 percent of the gains recorded in each calendar year are concentrated in a single 30-day period of time.* This means that if you review your account quarterly you will only have an average of one good quarter each year. The other quarters will be flat to down, on average. While this prospect seems unexciting, it's important because it is only through patient, long-term investing that you will realize your financial goals.

Small company stocks have enjoyed even better long-term performance than the large company stocks because of their higher risk. As indicated in Figure 10-2, small company stocks have grown at an average annual rate of 12.47 percent over the same 72-year period. Although these stocks are more volatile than large company stocks, the rewards have justified their higher risk. Also because small company stocks are more volatile than large company stocks, their returns are even more concentrated in short periods. Amazingly, *removing the best performing month in each calendar year reduces the total return from 12.47 percent to –1.90 percent!*

FIGURE 10-2

Growth of a Dollar without Highest Return Month

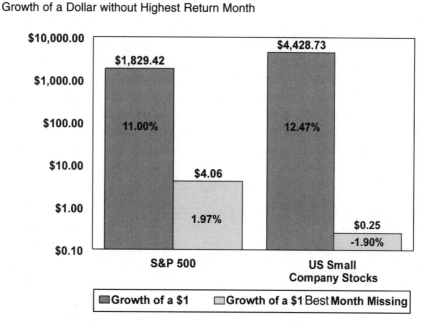

Source: Ibbotson Associates

FIGURE 10-3

Four Steps in a Quarterly Review

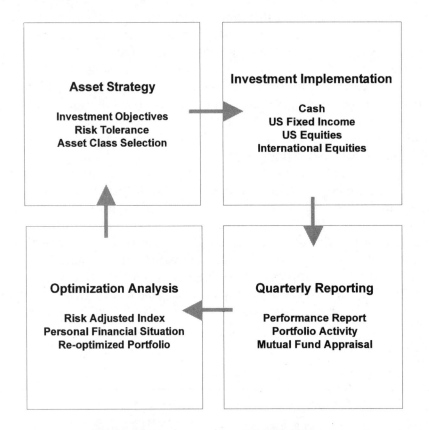

THE FOUR STEPS IN QUARTERLY REVIEWS

To deal with these ups and downs of the financial markets, you need a formal quarterly procedure that you can use to make sure you are staying on track. Figure 10-3 illustrates the four steps that we follow each quarter with our clients.

Step 1: Asset Strategy

The first step is to establish your asset strategy. You complete this step with your written investment policy statement. At a minimum, you must have clear investment objectives, have a suitable risk tolerance, and have identified the asset classes for inclusion in your portfolio. Each quarter you should review your portfolio to make sure that none of your investment guidelines have changed.

Step 2. Investment Implementation

Once your asset class strategy is completed, you are ready to implement your investment program. There are three questions you need to ask yourself:

1. Will I work with an investment advisor? If so, see Chapter 13 for advice on selecting an advisor.
2. Will I work directly with the mutual fund provider or with a broker-dealer that handles many mutual fund families?
3. Which specific asset class funds will I select? To assist in this process, see Chapter 6 for a list of currently available mutual funds.

Step 3. Quarterly Reporting

Each calendar quarter you should review your account. If you are working with a financial advisor, the advisor's report should clearly determine how the account has performed both for the portfolio as a whole and for each individual asset class. Portfolio activity—including trading, dividend payments, capital gain distributions, and fees—should also be included in this report.

If you are working on your own, you are responsible for reviewing your account statements and calculating the quarterly performance in each of the asset classes. Compare these reports with the expectations in your investment policy statement and against overall market benchmarks to make sure you are on track. If the performance is out of line with either measure there may be need for a change. You should be just as concerned about overperformance as underperformance. If the performance of one of your asset class mutual funds is different from its benchmark, it is likely that it is deviating from its asset class objectives and should be replaced.

Step 4. Optimization Analysis

We evaluate the efficiency of our clients' portfolios each quarter. Efficiency is measured by a risk-adjusted return index. This index measures the relative trade-off an investor is willing to accept as risk for an incremental increase in expected return. Fine-tuning trades are made when the account's risk-adjusted return index can be improved through reoptimization. If you are following the asset class strategy on your own, quarterly rebalancing to the original model portfolio should be considered. Be sure to include transaction costs in your calculations. For portfolios of less than $100,000, annual rebalancing is sufficient.

DOLLAR COST AVERAGING: DOES IT MAKE SENSE?

When we implement investment policies for clients who hold significant amounts of cash, the following question often arises: Is it better to make the transition to stocks immediately in one lump sum, or to use a dollar cost averaging strategy to invest in the market gradually, say in monthly or quarterly installments? Dollar cost averaging is not usually an issue for investors who are already invested in stocks; they are simply changing the composition of their equity holdings. Rather, it's the investors who are making the transition from cash to stocks who are fearful of investing all at once. They are afraid that the market will decline soon after they invest.

It seems that virtually every financial journalist and financial planner thinks dollar cost averaging is a good strategy to use. The usual argument made is that by investing an equal amount of money at regular intervals into a volatile asset, you will automatically buy more shares when the price is low and fewer shares when the price is high. Therefore, your average cost per share will always be less than the average price per share.

While this is an interesting mathematical fact, *it has no economic significance.* What is important is whether the shares that have been purchased can be sold for a gain. For this to happen, the average cost must be less than the current market price. Despite the widespread popularity of dollar cost averaging, there is no theoretical or empirical evidence that supports it. It seems, once again, that conventional investment wisdom is wrong.

There are many academic studies that prove dollar cost averaging is a suboptimal strategy. For example, George Constantinides of the University of Chicago uses a theoretical framework to show that dollar cost averaging is suboptimal.[1] Michael Rozeff comes to the same conclusion using computer simulation.[2] In another study, Peter Bacon and Richard Williams show that lump sum investing significantly outperforms dollar cost averaging nearly two-thirds of the time.[3] Williams and Bacon conclude that financial planners should encourage their clients to invest in the stock market as soon as possible. Mark Stumpp of Prudential Diversified Asset Management shares this view.[4] Over the period 1926 to 1994, he compares the results of buying the S&P 500 on the first day of January every year versus investing in 12 monthly installments. According to Stumpp, lump-sum in-

[1]Constantinides, G.M., "A Note of the Suboptimality of Dollar-Cost Averaging as an Investment Policy," *Journal of Quantitative Analysis* (June 1979), pp. 443–450.

[2]Rozeff, Michael, "Lump-Sum Investing Versus Dollar-Averaging," *Journal of Portfolio Management* (Winter 1994), pp. 45–50.

[3]Bacon, Peter and Richard Williams, "Lump-Sum Beats Dollar Cost Averaging," *Journal of Financial Planning* (April 1993), pp. 64–67.

[4]"The Dollar Cost Fallacy," *Forbes* (April 10, 1995), p. 59.

vesting beats dollar cost averaging by nearly four percentage points per year (12.2 percent versus 8.3 percent). Of course, dollar cost averaging is less risky than lump-sum investing, but the higher returns more than compensate for the increased volatility.[5]

Moreover, these studies only use one asset class. Lump-sum investing makes even more sense if you are investing in a well-diversified asset class portfolio, because you are buying into multiple asset categories rather than just one.

We believe dollar cost averaging remains popular despite all the evidence against it because it keeps investors from feeling remorseful about their decision to buy equities. Many investors prefer a dollar cost averaging strategy even though it reduces expected return. Lump-sum investing is unappealing because of the pain of regret investors would feel if stock prices crashed shortly after they invested. For financial planners, dollar cost averaging is simply good client relations. They'll never have a client angry with them for investing money in the market at the wrong time.

We do not recommend dollar cost averaging. It is a suboptimal strategy. If your investment policy statement calls for you to invest in stocks, you should take action immediately. Don't try to time the market or delay investing in stocks to avoid the pain of regret.

[5]Calculated by the Sharpe ratio, which is the excess average annual return over T-bills divided by the standard deviation.

11

Does Asset Class Investing Meet Investor Needs?

In this chapter, we will test the concepts of asset class investing one by one to determine whether asset class investing is successful in meeting the five basic needs outlined in Chapter 2.

INVESTOR NEED 1: DOES ASSET CLASS INVESTING REDUCE RISK?

While risk cannot be eliminated, it can be effectively controlled using the concepts of asset class investing. These strategies reduce risk and allow you to select a specific level of risk using historical data as a guide. You can then implement your allocation decisions using funds that deliver the results of those exact asset categories. No other method of investing allows you to design a portfolio precisely to a level of risk that corresponds exactly to the investment vehicles used in implementation.

Asset class performance data are available that allow investors to calculate the degree of correlation between different asset classes. As we discussed in Chapter 4, you can reduce risk by putting together a portfolio of asset classes with dissimilar price movements. For example, one asset class may move up, a second down, and a third not at all. The dissimilar movement of these different asset classes lessens short-term volatility.

Using dissimilar price movement diversification has another advantage. It enables you to take advantage of relatively high-risk, high-return asset classes within a conservative portfolio. This can be done as long as the high-risk asset class has a low correlation with the other assets in the portfolio. A good example is emerging market equities. They have high expected returns and high risk, but a low correlation with other asset classes.

Furthermore, asset class investing does not rely on subjective forecasts and the picking or timing ability of an active money manager. Those activities increase risk. Instead, you can rest assured that asset class investing will deliver market segment returns with reliability.

Table 11-1 illustrates the risk reduction benefits of effective diversification. Only the Global Equity Portfolio is more volatile than the S&P 500, and the Global Defensive and Global Conservative Portfolios have less risk than the Shearson Lehman Bond index, even though they have 25 percent and 50 percent stock exposure, respectively.

TABLE 11-1

Effective Diversification Risk Reduction

Index/Portfolio	Annual Standard Deviation 1972-1997
Global Defensive Portfolio	5.6%
Shearson Lehman Bond Index	7.9%
Global Conservative Portfolio	9.3%
Global Moderate Portfolio	12.7%
Global Aggressive Portfolio	15.3%
Standard & Poor's 500 Index	16.8%
Global Equity Portfolio	17.7%

INVESTOR NEED 2: DOES ASSET CLASS INVESTING INCREASE RETURNS?

All investors want to maximize returns with the least amount of risk. So how does asset class investing help you maximize your return on investment? In Chapter 4, we explain that two portfolios with the same average rate of return can have different compound rates of return. The portfolio that is less volatile will always have a higher compound rate of return and a higher ending wealth value. Asset class investing helps you capture this effect by targeting asset classes that do not move in tandem with each other.

CHAPTER 11

In addition, asset class investing allows you to fully participate in the free market's creation of wealth without all the costs associated with active management. On average, actively managed funds have underperformed asset class benchmarks due to their high operating expenses, which include management fees and trading costs. The lower costs of asset class funds increase your return dollar for dollar. Asset class investing is the most cost-effective way to invest today.

The returns of each of our model portfolios are illustrated in Figure 11-1.

FIGURE 11-1

Growth of a Dollar

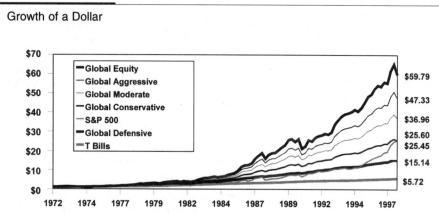

INVESTOR NEED 3: DOES ASSET CLASS INVESTING HELP INVESTORS REACH THEIR FINANCIAL GOALS?

In Chapter 10 we discussed the importance of developing your own investment policy statement, which involves knowing where you are now, where you want to go, and how you plan to get there. Reaching your financial goals is like running a business; you need to take a step back and look at the larger picture before you get started. Businesses fail primarily as a result of poor planning. Don't let this happen to you. To reach your financial goals successfully you need to plan first and establish a method to keep on course. Asset class investing gives you all the tools you need to be successful.

Many investors have poor results because they fall prey to the noise of the day. They become confused, make poor decisions, and get sidetracked. This is especially the case with investors who try to pick the top-performing funds. Due to the random nature of fund performance, their picks often do not perform according to their expectations. This causes frustration and encourages them to trade—severely hampering long-term returns and the likelihood of achieving their financial goals.

There will always be the temptation to follow conventional wisdom, particularly if you read the financial tabloids. You need to fight the urge to buy the hottest new mutual fund, the latest initial public offering, and Wall Street's "investment of the day." Asset class investing can help. It will insulate you from the day-to-day sensationalism sponsored by the media by providing a disciplined investment approach that focuses your attention on information rather than noise.

Asset class investing, together with your investment policy statement, will allow you to become an information investor who makes smart investment decisions. With asset class investing you have a plan to meet your objectives and the right tools with which to implement it.

INVESTOR NEED 4: DOES ASSET CLASS INVESTING PROVIDE A DEPENDABLE INCOME STREAM?

The reason most people invest today is to have spendable money tomorrow. Our investment strategy not only must be able to grow our capital, but also provide a steady income stream when we need it. Using our Global Conservative Portfolio as an example, let's see if asset class investing can provide a dependable income stream.

During the 26-year period from January 1, 1972 through December 31, 1997, U.S. Treasury bills earned an average annual rate of return of 6.9 percent. Over this same period, the Standard & Poor's 500 Index and the Global Conservative Portfolio each returned 13.3 percent. These percentages suggest that the safest way to invest for a steady income, and still have our investment portfolio grow, is to use the Global Conservative Portfolio or the S&P 500.

We assume that $100,000 is invested in each of three alternatives and that $2,000 per quarter is withdrawn from each investment.

Figure 11-2 shows that Treasury bills present the greatest problem for investors. They fail to earn a return high enough to pay out the income and maintain principal. The initial investment of $100,000 falls to $31,566 even before adjusting for inflation and taxes! The S&P 500 did better, with an ending value of $232,859, but this is not much reward for the significant risk taken due to lack of diversification.

Remarkably, even though the Global Conservative Portfolio is relatively low-risk, it finishes with an ending balance of $891,827! Why is there such a dramatic difference between the Global Conservative Portfolio and the S&P 500 when their average rates of return are almost the

FIGURE 11-2

Global Conservative vs. S&P 500 and T-Bills Less Quarterly Income of $2,000

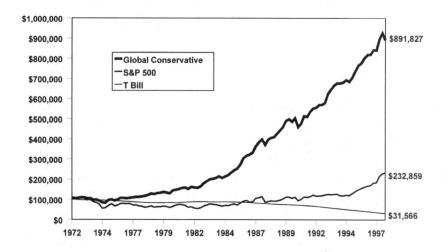

same? It has to do with volatility. The lower volatility of the Global Conservative Portfolio keeps it from being depleted too much in down markets. The severe market decline of 1973 and 1974 caused the S&P 500 to fall much further in value, from which it didn't recover. The continued income withdrawals during severe down periods make it difficult for a volatile, undiversified investment to rebound even after it recovers from its loss.

The most important message contained in this comparison is that a fixed-income vehicle is not necessary to provide a dependable income. Income investors should use diversified portfolios that include equities to generate the income they need. This total return approach will give investors the cash flow necessary to meet their income needs and keep pace with inflation. Asset class investing provides a prudent approach to the income dilemma.

INVESTOR NEED 5: DOES ASSET CLASS INVESTING PROVIDE LIQUIDITY?

Liquidity is the degree to which an asset can be liquidated quickly at current market values. Some investments, such as cash equivalents, are highly liquid. Others, such as directly held real estate, are very illiquid. Putting all their investments in a single asset class and then being forced to sell for liquidity reasons when that asset class was temporarily down in value has hurt many investors. Asset class investing reduces liquidity risk. Our model portfolios, for example, are comprised of equities from over 6,000 different stocks in 24 different countries. It is unlikely that they would all be down at the same time. Asset class funds, like all no-load funds, can be liquidated at full net asset value at the close of trading on any given day.

A prudent investor should typically maintain cash reserves equal to six month's worth of expenses, as well as a provision for any large expenditure planned over the next five years. These funds should be invested in short-term fixed income securities with low volatility. No funds should be invested in an asset class portfolio unless they can be committed to a longer-term time horizon.

When an unexpected need for liquidity arises, consideration should be given to using a margin loan to obtain the funds. This will not disrupt the portfolio, create transaction costs and taxes, or cause you to change your allocation. The cost of margin loans is very competitive and often can be negotiated. The maximum amount available is 50 percent of the market value of your account. A margin loan should only be used when you can pay it off within a short period, say six months.

In summary, asset class investing allows prudent investors to meet all their investor needs.

Asset class investing makes traditional investments obsolete. In Chapter 12, we'll put together your asset class portfolio and get you started.

TABLE 11-2

Investor Needs

	Yes	No
Risk Reduction	X	
Return Enhancement	X	
Strategy to Achieve Specific Financial Objectives	X	
Dependable Income Stream	X	
Ability to Liquidate Quickly	X	

CHAPTER

Putting It All Together

You are now ready to build your own asset class portfolio. In this chapter, we show you how to use each of the five key concepts and outline the steps necessary to construct your own investment program. First, we review each of the key concepts that you should incorporate in your portfolio. Then we compare how the introduction of each new asset class fund incrementally adds value, ultimately increasing returns by over 3 percent per year compared to a traditional mutual fund portfolio.

KEY CONCEPTS TO INCORPORATE INTO YOUR PORTFOLIO

Concept 1: Utilize diversification effectively to reduce risk

The ideal investment allows investors to financially meet their goals and objectives while sleeping well at night. Effective diversification can take you a long way toward reaching this goal.

We have learned from the work of Harry Markowitz, the Nobel Prize winner in economics, that there are two kinds of diversification: effective diversification and ineffective diversification. If you have many different investments but they tend to move together, you have ineffective diversification. It's as if you didn't diversify at all. However, if your investments do not move in tandem, you will gain diversification benefits from the dissimilar price movements. As you now know, this allows the risk of the total portfolio to be less than the average risk of its components. We have carefully chosen each of the asset class building blocks we use in this chapter as well as in our model portfolios to implement this concept of risk reduction.

Concept 2: Dissimilar price movement diversification enhances return

To the extent you take advantage of effective diversification, you will increase the expected rate of return of your portfolio. You learned in Chapter 4 that if two portfolios have the same average return, the one with less volatility will have a greater compound return. In building your asset class portfolio you not only reduce risk but also enhance returns through effective diversification.

Concept 3: Employ asset class investing

To build your portfolio you need cost-effective building blocks that make use of these concepts. Asset class funds are designed to meet these goals, as we discussed in Chapter 6. Since they are passively managed, asset class funds do not actively buy and sell securities to try to take advantage of subjective forecasts. They recognize that markets are efficient and that the best way for them to add value is to provide cost-effective representation of a particular asset class. Asset class funds are designed to be the building blocks of effectively diversified portfolios.

Concept 4: Global diversification reduces risk

As you learned in Chapter 7, investing in many different countries allows you to reduce risk and enhance returns with an additional dimension of diversification. Most of the stocks of a single country tend to be highly correlated with each other. With the introduction of international asset classes you gain greater downside protection by spreading your bets across different markets that have a low correlation with each other.

Concept 5: Design portfolios that are efficient

Your portfolio should be designed to provide you with the highest return for the level of risk with which you are comfortable. In Chapter 8, we showed you the math behind these concepts and our five model portfolios that fall within the range of the efficient frontier. One of these portfolios is probably right for you.

BUILDING AN ASSET CLASS PORTFOLIO—ONE ASSET CLASS AT A TIME

In this section we build an asset class portfolio to show you how asset class investing adds value beyond conventional investment strategies. We do this by comparing the results an average investor might have achieved from January 1976 through December 1997, with the results of an asset class portfolio built according to the principles described in this book.

Step 1. The 60–40 Investor

We begin with a traditional, balanced portfolio allocation: 60 percent stocks and 40 percent bonds (see Figure 12-1).

We assume that an investor invests $100,000 in January 1976 in a combined portfolio equal to 60 percent in the average return of all equity mutual funds and 40 percent in the average return of all bond mutual funds on the Morningstar database. The investor would have earned the average rate of return on the investments through December 1997 shown in Table 12-1.

FIGURE 12-1

60% Equity Funds—40% Bond Funds

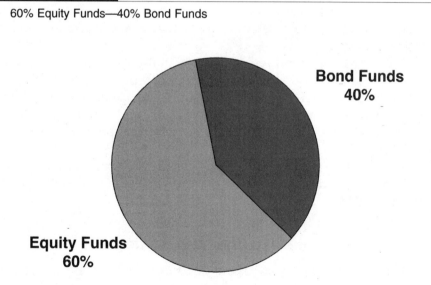

TABLE 12-1

Portfolio	Years	Average Compound Return %	Standard Deviation % (Risk)	Growth of $1
60% Equity Funds, 40% Bond Funds	22	13.55	10.18	16.37

An investment made on January 1, 1976 would have earned a compound rate of return of 13.55 percent with a standard deviation of 10.18 percent. A dollar would have grown to $16.37. This is the benchmark with which we will compare the asset class investing strategies you have learned, even though it overstates returns for several reasons.

First, most investors would not have been able to stay invested for such a long period of time without second-guessing whether they were in the best mutual funds or questioning whether they should be in the stock market at all. Many would have changed their portfolios several times over this 22-year period, chasing after hot funds and moving in and out of the market.

Second, income taxes would have significantly reduced investors' returns, if the investments were held in taxable accounts. This occurs because of the high turnover of most retail mutual funds, as well as fund switching by investors themselves, activity that would cause the realization of taxable capital gains.

Third, the average fund returns we use in this example are artificially high because of survivorship bias. Many poorly performing funds have been terminated or merged into more successful funds. The poor performers no longer show up on the Morningstar fund database, therefore the returns of the survivors, and of our hypothetical portfolio, are artificially high.

Even though this benchmark overstates the performance of the average investor, it provides a starting point from which to measure the added value of asset class investing.

Step 2. The Indexed Portfolio

If you had used the two most basic index funds—60 percent in the S&P 500 index and 40 percent in the Shearson Lehman Intermediate Bond index—you would have earned about the same rate of return, but with less risk.

FIGURE 12-2

60% S&P 500—40% S/L Inter. Bonds

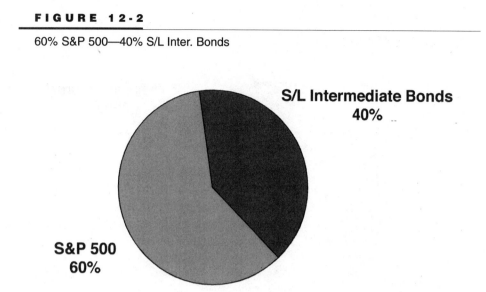

TABLE 12-2

Portfolio	Years	Average Compound Return %	Standard Deviation % (Risk)	Growth of $1
60% Equity Funds, 40% Bond Funds	22	13.55	10.18	16.37
60% S&P 500 Index, 40% S/L Bond Index	22	13.33	9.53	15.69

In steps 3 through 6, we will add asset classes using simple percentage allocations to demonstrate how asset class investing can add significant value to your portfolio.

Step 3. Substitute Short-Term Fixed Income

Substituting short-term fixed income for intermediate-term bonds reduces risk without reducing returns. In this example, we have replaced the Shearson Lehman Intermediate Bond Index, which has a weighted average maturity of 3.5 to 4.5 years, with a two-year fixed income asset class fund. This asset class fund uses the matrix pricing strategy discussed in Chapter 6. The reduction in fixed income risk allows you to invest more heavily in higher-risk, higher-expected-return equities without exceeding your risk tolerance level. This is one way to increase returns without increasing overall risk.

FIGURE 12-3

Shorten Fixed Maturities

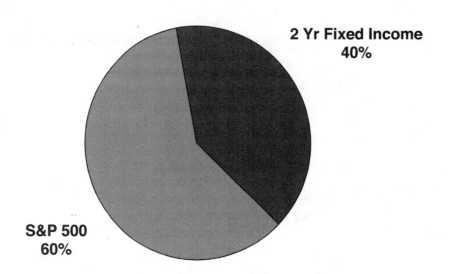

2 Yr Fixed Income
40%

S&P 500
60%

TABLE 12-3

Portfolio	Years	Average Compound Return %	Standard Deviation % (Risk)	Growth of $1
60% Equity Funds, 40% Bond Funds	22	13.55	10.18	16.37
60% S&P 500 Index, 40% S/L Bond Index	22	13.33	9.53	15.69
Shorten Fixed Maturities	*22*	*13.30*	*8.72*	*15.59*

Step 4. Introduce the Size Effect

Researchers have found that investors demand higher compensation for investing in small company stocks. We call this the size effect. In fact, small stocks have delivered higher long-term returns worldwide, in every market studied.

In this step, we reduce our allocation to each of the large company asset classes by one-third and reallocate it to small stocks both in the U.S. and overseas. The introduction of this risky asset class increases annual returns by more than 1 percent, with only a .5 percent increase in overall portfolio volatility. This is so because small company stocks are not perfectly correlated with large company stocks and they have a very low correlation with short-term debt instruments.

FIGURE 12-4

Introduce Size Effect

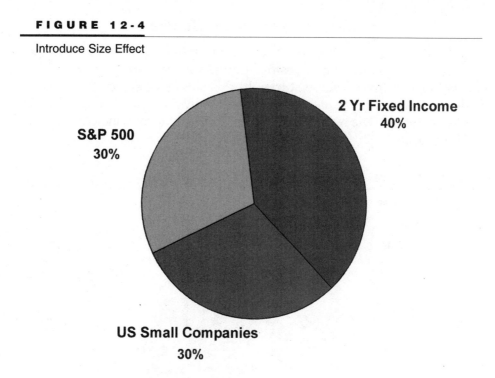

S&P 500
30%

2 Yr Fixed Income
40%

US Small Companies
30%

TABLE 12-4

Portfolio	Years	Average Compound Return %	Standard Deviation % (Risk)	Growth of $1
60% Equity Funds, 40% Bond Funds	22	13.55	10.18	16.37
60% S&P 500 Index, 40% S/L Bond Index	22	13.33	9.53	15.69
Shorten Fixed Maturities	22	13.30	8.72	15.59
Introduce Size Effect	*22*	*14.40*	*9.22*	*19.31*

Step 5. Add Value Stocks

The third risk factor is the value factor, measured by the book-to-market ratio. Research shows that investors around the world demand higher returns for investing in value stocks. In this step, we replace the S&P 500 index with U.S. large value stocks as defined by the work of Eugene Fama and Ken French. The result is higher returns with a small increase in portfolio volatility.

FIGURE 12-5

Add Value Stocks

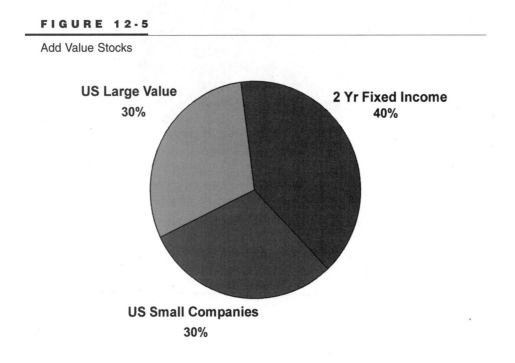

US Large Value
30%

2 Yr Fixed Income
40%

US Small Companies
30%

TABLE 12-5

Portfolio	Years	Average Compound Return %	Standard Deviation % (Risk)	Growth of $1
60% Equity Funds, 40% Bond Funds	22	13.55	10.18	16.37
60% S&P 500 Index, 40% S/L Bond Index	22	13.33	9.53	15.69
Shorten Fixed Maturities	22	13.30	8.72	15.59
Introduce Size Effect	22	14.40	9.22	19.31
Add Value Stocks	22	15.10	9.60	22.06

CHAPTER 12

FIGURE 12-6

Diversify Globally

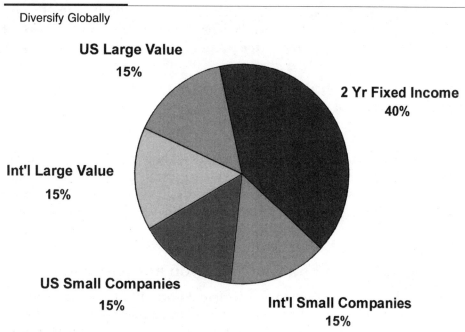

TABLE 12-6

Portfolio	Years	Average Compound Return %	Standard Deviation % (Risk)	Growth of $1
60% Equity Funds, 40% Bond Funds	22	13.55	10.18	16.37
60% S&P 500 Index, 40% S/L Bond Index	22	13.33	9.53	15.69
Shorten Fixed Maturities	22	13.30	8.72	15.59
Introduce Size Effect	22	14.40	9.22	19.31
Add Value Stocks	22	15.10	9.60	22.06
Diversify Globally	22	15.47	8.83	23.66

Step 6. Diversify Globally

Foreign markets and domestic markets do not move in tandem with each other. Therefore, international investments can increase returns while reducing risk. In this step, we add global diversification by diversifying 30 percent of our portfolio into foreign equities.

Asset class investing adds value by allowing you to effectively diversify both across and within asset categories, and allowing you to fully capture the returns delivered by global capital markets. You can do all of this without the cost and uncertain results of conventional investment strategies.

In our 22-year example, asset class investing increased returns by nearly 2 percent per year, and significantly increased the growth of a dollar invested from $16.37 to $23.66. This represents more than a 45 percent increase in the ending wealth of the portfolio over our benchmark.

GETTING A QUICK START ON YOUR OWN ASSET CLASS PORTFOLIO

Step 1: Identify your investment fund

Use financial planning techniques to figure out how much money you can invest for long-term goals in a diversified portfolio. This is the amount you should start with. Invest it in your portfolio all at once, without dollar cost averaging. The sooner you invest your money, the more time it will have to grow.

Step 2: Decide how much risk you are willing to take

Use historical data to examine how different portfolios have performed in bad markets. Make sure that you can withstand a market decline like the one from 1973 through 1974. To be successful in the long run you must stay fully invested without wavering in the short run. Don't underestimate how difficult this can be. If you decide to work with an advisor, he or she well help you through this modeling process and be there to reinforce your asset class investing strategy in both good times and bad.

Step 3: Consider using one of our model portfolios

This will keep things simple and prevent "paralysis by analysis." Don't overanalyze. Select the portfolio that most closely aligns with your risk tolerance and return objectives.

Step 4: Select the most appropriate asset class funds

Choose funds that most cost-effectively incorporate the concepts that we have discussed. In Chapter 6, we list many of the currently available pure index and asset class mutual funds. If you work with an advisor, you will have access to institutional funds that offer advantages over most retail funds. Measure your funds' performance against appropriate benchmarks on a regular basis.

Step 5: Rebalance you account at least annually

By systematically rebalancing to your original allocation you will sell those asset classes that have gone up the most and buy those that have lagged. This discipline eliminates the negative results of emotional trading and helps maintain the portfolio's risk profile.

MORE PROOF THAT ASSET CLASS INVESTING WORKS: PERFORMANCE OF THE MODEL PORTFOLIOS

In Table 12-7 we compare how the five model portfolios would have performed relative to all balanced, retail mutual funds that have been in existence from January 1975 through December 1997. It is easy to see that asset class investing adds value.

Asset class investing is not easy. Most people don't have the time, knowledge, or discipline to do it themselves. They prefer to work with a professional financial advisor to help them with their asset class investing strategy. A good professional can add substantial value. In Chapter 13, we examine the pros and cons of working with an advisor and discuss how to find one who is right for you.

TABLE 12-7

Performance of the Model Portfolios (January 1972-December 1997)

Fund Name	Annualized Return	Annualized Std. Dev.
1. Global Equity	18.49	14.51
2. Global Aggressive	17.08	12.50
3. Global Moderate	15.63	10.46
4. Merrill Lynch Capital A	15.48	9.41
5. Fidelity Puritan	15.42	9.97
6. State Farm Balanced	15.32	10.15
7. Vanguard/Wellington	15.23	10.51
8. Dodge & Cox Balanced	14.91	9.67
9. CGM Mutual	14.65	13.81
10. MFS Total Return A	14.33	8.45
11. Vanguard/Wellesley Income	14.02	7.75
12. American Balanced	14.00	8.48
13. Phoenix Income & Growth A	13.92	8.14
14. IDS Mutual A	13.76	9.07
15. United Continental Income A	13.64	9.54
16. Global Conservative	13.52	7.67
17. George Putnam of Boston A	13.43	9.40
18. T. Rowe Price Balanced	13.30	7.75
19. Alliance Balanced Shares A	13.21	11.22
20. Franklin Income I	13.20	7.81
21. Delaware A	13.16	9.97
22. Founders Balanced	13.14	8.55
23. Sentinel Balanced A	13.08	8.03
24. Pax World	13.07	8.01
25. Federated Stock & Bond A	12.73	7.56
26. Kemper Total Return A	12.72	11.38
27. Keystone Balanced (K-1)	12.57	9.18
28. United Retirement Shares A	12.50	9.53
29. Composite Bond & Stock A	12.46	8.18
30. Stein Roe Balanced	12.33	9.25
31. New England Balanced A	12.02	11.41
32. Pioneer Balanced A	11.06	6.63
33. Global Defensive	10.68	4.37

13

How to Select a Financial Advisor

In this chapter, we uncover why so many investors feel uncomfortable working with investment professionals. We'll show you how to evaluate whether it makes sense for you to use a financial advisor and, if so, how to select your investment advisory team.

WHY ARE SO MANY INVESTORS UNCOMFORTABLE WORKING WITH INVESTMENT PROFESSIONALS?

We recently asked our investors about their concerns in reaching their financial goals. They shared four major issues with us. Asset class investing provides a solution to all four.

1. The most common issue is that investors feel uncomfortable with the financial services industry in general due to the transactional nature of the business. They view the industry's traditional commission-based pay structure as a conflict of interest. Until recently, unless your investment assets totaled over $1 million, it was very difficult to hire a competent, fee-based financial advisor. For this reason, most individual investors have been forced to work with financial salespeople—stockbrokers, insurance agents, or financial planners—who are paid commissions by investment product sponsors. Investors are suspect of the recommendations they receive from these sources. The problem is that commissioned salespeople are paid to sell products rather than to solve problems.

In comparison, financial advisors who specialize in asset class investing are paid a predetermined fee, not a commission. This fee is usually a percentage of assets under management and is paid as you go. Therefore, the advisor has to provide you with high-quality service to keep your account. Since the fee is linked to the size of your account, the advisor makes more money as your account increases in value. This aligns your interests because you both want your account to grow. A traditional commissioned salesperson, on the other hand, earns compensation up front on the initial transaction, and has little financial incentive to provide you with good service after the sale. This is not a logical way to pay for financial services.

2. The second strongest concern for investors is that they feel unsure of how they are doing. They have a hard time understanding the information on their monthly brokerage statements, and tracking performance is particularly troublesome for investors with multiple accounts. Moreover, individual investors must keep track of their cost basis for tax purposes, a task that is getting more challenging with every major tax change.

   A good financial advisor will solve these problems and keep you up to date on your portfolio's performance. Most send quarterly performance reports and will meet with you regularly to make sure you are fully informed. The advisor will also keep track of tax basis information and ensure that sales are accounted for tax-effectively, based on current tax laws.

3. The third most common concern is that there is so much noise—in the form of contradictory advice, media hype, and information overload—that investors easily get confused and then don't feel comfortable taking any action. A knowledgeable and experienced advisor can help investors filter out the noise and determine what is useful information.

4. The fourth concern expressed is the fear that decisions will be made for emotional reasons rather than as part of a well-defined, academically sound approach. Financial advisors who utilize asset class investing follow a disciplined investment approach that is rooted in academic knowledge.

WHAT ARE THE ADVANTAGES OF WORKING WITH A FINANCIAL ADVISOR?

There are four main advantages to having an advisor help you put your asset class investing program together.

Advantage 1: Time savings

Time has become a scarce resource in today's rapid-paced world. Few people have enough time to do all the things they want to do. An advisor can do much of the work of drafting your investment policy statement, implementing it, and reviewing your portfolio on a quarterly basis. Most investors, even if they are inclined to manage their money themselves, don't have the time do so properly. They find it cost-effective to hire a professional advisor and spend more time themselves on other financially rewarding work or activities.

Advantage 2: Institutional funds

Advisors often have access to institutional asset class mutual funds that are not available to the public. These institutional asset class funds provide investors with the following benefits:

- low expenses,
- exposure to unique, high-expected-return asset categories,
- enhanced trading strategies, and
- institutional ownership.

Unlike retail funds, which are generally stand-alone investments, institutional asset class funds are designed to be put together in a portfolio by an investment professional. They function as highly sophisticated building blocks for prudent asset class investors.

Advantage 3: Discipline

Money is a very emotional subject for most people. It can be hard to make emotionally detached, rational decisions regarding one's own money. A financial advisor can solve this problem by bringing objectivity to financial decision making. An advisor can help investors make difficult decisions and stay objective during times of stress. Discipline is one of the most important elements of successful investing.

Advantage 4: Knowledge

Most individual investors do not have the training required to be effective investors on their own. There is an ever-increasing body of knowledge that must be thoroughly understood if one is to be a self-sufficient investor. Gathering this knowledge and staying up to date is time-consuming and costly. Few investors are willing to make this kind of commitment.

A qualified advisor has spent years in formal training, learning about how markets work and how to apply their knowledge for their clients' benefit. In addition, advisors who have professional credentials must fulfill regular continuing education requirements. Most also have access to information that is not available to individuals. This information can help them to make better, more informed recommendations to their clients.

HOW TO SELECT YOUR INVESTMENT ADVISORY TEAM

An investment advisory team normally consists of two members: a financial advisor and a money management firm. The financial advisor is generally an independent professional whose only motive should be to represent the clients' best interests. The advisor will work with you to write and implement your investment policy statement and will review your account with you on a quarterly basis. A money management firm with the capability to manage your portfolio is normally used to implement asset class strategies, although some advisors choose to manage portfolios themselves.

QUALIFICATIONS YOU SHOULD SEEK IN YOUR MONEY MANAGEMENT FIRM

There are five qualifications you should look for in a money management firm.[1]

1. **Independence.** The money management firm should not be engaged in, affiliated with, or controlled by any organization in the brokerage, insurance, underwriting, or other financial services fields. It should not be owned or organized in any way that could jeopardize its ability to render independent advice.

2. **Investment Philosophy.** The money management firm should have a consistent philosophy that does not confuse investing with trading or speculating. It should consistently follow its

[1]Babson, D., "The Commercial and Financial Chronicle" (June 28, 1973, pp. 12-13; as excerpted by C. Ellis, *Classics II: Another Investor's Anthology* (Business One Irwin, 1991), pp. 550–551.

investment philosophy—in bad as well as in good years, and under all types of economic and political conditions. This shows that it has the commitment and discipline to follow its philosophy.

3. **Specialization.** The money management firm should not be a financial department store. Its efforts should be primarily engaged in investment analysis and portfolio management, rather than spread out over a whole range of unrelated activities.

4. **Teamwork.** A diversely talented and experienced staff that works closely together is more likely to produce effective results than either the superstar system or a big, loosely knit organization whose internal communications are cumbersome and often inconsistent.

5. **Integrity.** The money management firm should be committed to the highest levels of ethical standards and honesty, and regard its services as a serious trust. They should put their clients' needs first, stand behind their work, and deliver on their promises.

You should only consider working with a money management firm that can meet these five qualifications. Of course, the firm's investment philosophy must be consistent with the principles of asset class investing and your new understanding of how markets work. The best way to find a good money manager is through a financial advisor—but not just any financial advisor. The next section tells you why you should select an advisor.

WHY A FINANCIAL ADVISOR?

Unfortunately, most financial professionals are ill-equipped to assist you with asset class investing. This includes insurance salespeople, stockbrokers, and tax advisors who have changed their titles to financial planner to gain a marketing advantage. Often, these individuals want to sell you a product, rather than help you make smart financial decisions. This is not the fault of these professionals; the commission-based pay structure of the industry sets up a conflict of interest.

The good news is that a good financial advisor can have a significant impact on your investment success. Let's look at one study completed by Dalbar Financial Services, Inc. to see how much value an advisor can add. This study shows the total returns earned by individual investors who invested on their own using directly marketed investment products, compared to those who worked with a financial advisor. We have also included the model portfolios' results for the same time period, so you can see the substantial benefits of asset class investing.

TABLE 13-1

Dalbar Results and Model Portfolios (January 1984–September 1993)

	Total Return %	Annual Standard Deviation %
Dalbar Results		
Investors on their Own	70.23	n/a
Investors with Advisors	90.21	n/a
Model Portfolios		
Global Defensive	258.98	6.60
Global Conservative	374.44	10.10
Global Moderate	462.99	13.00
Global Aggressive	549.07	16.00
Global Equity	708.45	17.30

Source: Dalbar, 1994.

The results: From January 1984 through September 1993, investors using a financial advisor realized total returns of 90.21 percent versus 70.23 percent for the do-it-yourself investors (see Table 13-1). This is about a 2 percent per year advantage for the investors with advisors. The study concludes that individuals who go it alone are more likely to try to time markets rather than hold assets for the long term.

The Dalbar study confirms what we have known for a long time: On average, individuals managing their own money lack the training and discipline necessary to reach their financial goals. This builds a pretty good case for working with an advisor.

Unfortunately, most financial advisors do not understand the concepts featured in this book, or they simply choose to ignore them. As we have learned, most financial advisors attempt to add value by trying to pick securities—or worse, by telling you which way the market's going and whether to get in or out. They follow traditional investment strategies that we now know don't make sense theoretically or empirically. It is critical for you to find a knowledgeable advisor who understands asset class investing to ensure that you reach your financial goals. Next, we discuss where to find a financial advisor and what questions to ask.

WHERE TO FIND A FINANCIAL ADVISOR

Most people find their financial advisors through referrals. These referrals usually come from friends, coworkers, accountants, or attorneys. Although this is a comfortable method for most people, it has two major pitfalls. First, in today's litigious society, professionals and laypeople alike are less willing to refer you to others due to the implied endorsement. This is especially true of accountants and attorneys. They simply don't want to take the risk that you will have a bad experience and hold them at fault. Second, most people don't understand the concepts within this book. Third, people often make a referral because they like an advisor personally, but they are not qualified to judge an advisor's skill and knowledge of investing.

Referrals are a good place to start, but you've got to do your homework. Ask any potential advisor plenty of questions. Most important, make sure the advisor satisfies the qualifications listed in the next section. If you want help in identifying a financial professional in your area who offers asset class investing, call our office at 1-800-366-7266. Ask for a list of qualified financial advisors in your area.

QUALIFICATIONS YOU SHOULD EXPECT FROM YOUR FINANCIAL ADVISOR

- Your advisor should construct portfolios according to the principles of Modern Portfolio Theory. He or she should understand and agree that markets are efficient and that asset allocation decisions, rather than security selection and market timing, determine the majority of investment results. The advisor should build portfolios that capture diversification benefits and favorable risk-return characteristics.
- The advisor should be compensated on a fee-only basis rather than through brokerage commissions. Advisors who work on commissions are more likely to recommend frequent transactions in your portfolio. A fee-only advisor has fewer conflicts of interest and is more likely to have your best interests in mind.
- The advisor should focus on risk in selecting your portfolio. Reviewing historical portfolio performance in bad markets is the best way to get a feel for the potential volatility of a particular asset mix. Paying attention to risk will give you the best chance of staying invested throughout your time horizon, because your portfolio will be consistent with your risk tolerance.
- The advisor should work with you to set target rates of return— the returns you will need to achieve your objectives. A fee-only advisor can show you different models and mixes of investments that have the highest probability of achieving your goals.
- The advisor should write an investment policy statement for you. The statement should provide specific instructions covering the following objectives and constraints: target return, risk tolerance,

time horizon, anticipated withdrawals or contributions, tax constraints, and regulatory issues, if any.

- The advisor should purchase selected asset classes of institutional asset class mutual funds. These funds have several advantages over retail mutual funds, such as lower operating expenses, lower trading costs, lower turnover rates, and consistent asset allocation.
- The advisor should rebalance your portfolio periodically. If an asset differs significantly from its original target allocation, the advisor should either buy or sell some of the asset until its target percentage is restored.
- Your advisor should provide you with a quarterly assessment of the portfolio's performance and market values. He or she should determine whether the market value of your portfolio is growing quickly enough to achieve your objectives and whether any adjustments need to be made.

Some investors and inexperienced advisors believe that once they build an asset class portfolio, they won't need to make any changes. If we look back just five years, we see that asset class investing has improved dramatically. Researchers have identified new asset classes, leading to the development of many new asset class funds. Value and emerging market funds are two recent introductions.

Over the next five years, it is likely that we will see even greater changes. It would be foolish for any investor not to take advantage of new knowledge and products. Finding an advisor to help you keep informed of new developments will add tremendous value to your portfolio.

We wish you the best of success with your asset class investing. You have earned it! We welcome your written comments on this book. Feel free to write or email us.

John Bowen

Reinhardt Werba Bowen Advisory Services
1190 Saratoga Avenue
Suite 200
San Jose, CA 95129
jbowen@rwb.com

Dan Goldie

Reinhardt Werba Bowen Advisory Services
150 Portola Road
Portola Valley, CA 94028

dgoldie@rwb.com

Formulas

EXPECTED RATES OF RETURN

Cash and Equivalents

The first fixed income asset class is cash and equivalents. In our portfolios we use a money market fund for this asset category. It is simply the current 90-day Treasury bill rate. An alternative is to use the current yield on the money market fund you are considering using.

The expected rate of return is calculated as follows:

$R_{mm} = t_{90}$

where

R_{mm} = Money market expected return

t_{90} = Observed 90-day Treasury bill return

Short-Term Fixed Income

The second fixed income asset class is short-term fixed income. We use a two-year corporate fixed income portfolio for our clients. This asset class's expected rate of return is equal to the current 30-day Treasury bill rate plus a premium for maturity and a matrix pricing strategy that shifts maturities in response to changes in the shape of the yield curve.

The expected rate of return is calculated as follows:

$R_f = t_{30} + P_t$

where

R_f = Two-year corporate expected return

t_{30} = Observed 30-day Treasury bill return

P_t = Observed premium of two-year corporate fixed income
strategy over 30-day Treasury bill.

Large Company Value Stocks

Since the expected rates of return are the same for value stocks of equal size around the world, we use the same expected return for domestic and foreign large value stocks.

The expected rate of return for large value stocks is equal to the current risk-free rate plus a premium for market and value risk. Over long periods of time, investors are rewarded on average for owning securities that are sensitive to both of these risk factors. In the short run, however, return differentials for market or value risk can be negative.

The expected rate of return for this asset class is calculated as follows:

$$R_{lv} = t_{30} + P_e + P_v$$

where

R_{lv} = Large company value stocks expected return

t_{30} = Observed 30-day Treasury bill return

P_e = Observed premium of S&P 500 index over 30-day Treasury bill

P_v = Observed premium of Fama and French value index over S&P 500 index

Small Company Stocks

Small company stocks have higher expected returns than large company stocks. Investors would not buy small company stocks if they had the same returns as large companies. They must be enticed by higher returns to buy more risky securities. Small companies are subject to downturns in times of recession and their stock prices are highly volatile. Their risk is substantially higher than large stocks and investors need to be rewarded for the increased risk. As with large stocks, the expected size premium is the same for small stocks around the world.

The expected return for small company stocks is equal to the current risk-free rate plus a premium for market risk and a premium for size risk.

The expected return is:

$$R_{sc} = t_{30} + P_e + P_s$$

where

R_{sc} = Small company stocks expected return

t_{30} = Observed 30-day Treasury bill return

P_e = Observed premium of S&P 500 index over the 30-day Treasury bill return

P_s = Observed small company return (CRSP 9th and 10th deciles) over the S&P 500 index

Emerging Market Stocks

In calculating expected rates of return we want to use as long a time series of information as possible. Unfortunately, the time series data on emerging markets are very short. We are forced to make estimates of expected returns due to the lack of empirical data.

Emerging market stocks have characteristics of both market and size risk factors. They are generally large companies that are headquartered in small countries. Therefore, we believe it is reasonable to assume that emerging market stocks should have similar return characteristics to those of mid-cap stocks.

The expected return for emerging market stocks is equal to the current risk-free rate plus a premium for market risk plus one-half the premium for size risk.

The expected rate of return is calculated as follows:

$$R_{em} = t_{30} + P_e + (.5 \times P_s)$$

where

R_{em} = Emerging market stocks expected return

t_{30} = Observed 30-day Treasury bill return

P_e = Observed premium of S&P 500 index over the 30-day Treasury bill return

P_s = Observed small company return (CRSP 9th and 10th deciles) over the S&P 500 index

STANDARD DEVIATION

Standard deviation measures the risk or return volatility of an individual security or portfolio. The formula for the standard deviation of an individual security is:

$$\sigma = \sqrt{\frac{(X_1 - \overline{X})^2 + (X_2 - \overline{X})^2 + \ldots + (X_N - \overline{X})^2}{N}}$$

Standard Deviation = Square Root of Variance

$$\text{Variance} = \frac{(X_1 - \overline{X})^2 + (X_2 - \overline{X})^2 + \ldots + (X_N - \overline{X})^2}{N}$$

where

$\overline{X}$ = Average value of the variable for the period observed

N = Number of observations[1]

---

[1]Purists will divide by N–1 instead of N to ensure that the estimate of variance is an unbiased estimate of the true or underlying variance.

To determine the standard deviation for each of the asset classes, we have used their historical standard deviation. With any statistical measure we suggest using the longest time series available, unless there are valid reasons for discarding certain information. Many publications use short periods in calculating the standard deviation, such as three, five, or even ten years. We don't think these relatively short periods of time allow for sufficient understanding of the true risk of an asset class.

CORRELATION COEFFICIENT

The formula to determine the correlation coefficient between two asset classes is the covariance between X and Y = Average of $(X - \overline{X})(Y - \overline{Y})$

$$\text{Correlation} = \frac{\overline{(X_1 - \overline{X})^2 + (X_2 - \overline{X})}}{(\sigma_X)(\sigma_Y)}$$

A portfolio's expected rate of return is simply the weighted average expected return of each of its components. The standard deviation of a portfolio, however, is not the weighted average of its components. A portfolio's standard deviation is reduced from a simple weighted average to the extent its assets do not move in tandem, as measured by the correlation coefficients of its assets. A portfolio's variance is:

Portfolio variance = $w_1^2 s_1^2 + 2 w_1 w_2 r_{12} s_1 s_2 + w_2^2 s_2^2$

where

$w_1, 2_2$ = Proportion of the portfolio invested in assets 1 and 2

s_1, s_2 = Standard deviations of returns on assets 1 and 2

r_{12} = Correlations between returns on assets 1 and 2

SINGLE-FACTOR MODEL (CAPM)

$R(t) - RF(t) = \alpha + \beta[RM(t) - RF(t) + r(t)]$

Average expected return minus Treasury bill = average excess return + beta [market return] minus Treasury bill.

This model explains 70 percent of the variability of returns based on average three-factor model explanatory power (R^2) for the Fama and French equity benchmark universe.

THREE-FACTOR MODEL

$R(t) - RF(t) = \alpha + \beta[RM(t) - RF(t)] + sSMB(t) + hHML(t) + e(t)$

Average expected return minus Treasury bill = average excess return + beta [market return] minus Treasury bill + sensitivity to size [small stocks minus big stocks] + sensitivity to BTM [high BTM minus low BTM].

This model explains 95 percent of the variability of returns based on average three-factor model explanatory power (R^2) for the Fama and French equity benchmark universe.

Index

About the Authors

John J. Bowen, Jr.

John is President and CEO of Reinhardt Werba Bowen Advisory Services, an investment advisory firm with more than $1.5 billion in assets under management.

John has written two books, *The Prudent Investor's Guide to Beating the Market,* Irwin (1995), which he coauthored, and *Creating Equity,* Securities Data Publishing (1997). John's expertise as a financial advisor has lead to appearances on CNBC, CNN and Bloomberg, and he is often quoted in the *Wall Street Journal, USA Today,* and *U.S. News & World Report.*

John is a member of the advisory board for the *Journal of Practice Management* and writes a monthly column in *Financial Planning* magazine. He has taught several courses on investment theory for the MBA program at Golden Gate University, and similar courses for other colleges throughout the San Francisco Bay Area.

A Certified Financial Planner (CFP) and Registered Securities Principal, John is also President of Reinhardt Werba Bowen Securities, Inc., a registered NASD broker/dealer. He is a member of the International Association for Financial Planning and on the Board of Advisors of the Institute for Investment Management Consultants.

John received a Bachelor of Science degree in Economics from the State University of New York, a Master of Business Administration degree in Taxation from Golden Gate University, and a Master of Science degree in Financial Services from the American College.

Daniel C. Goldie

Dan is Senior Financial Advisor for Reinhardt Werba Bowen Advisory Services where he oversees $100 million of client assets. He has written several articles and white papers for the firm, and is a frequent speaker at investment workshops and educational seminars. He has presented the concepts of investment theory, asset allocation, and asset class investing to a variety of audiences, including the general public, investment clubs, retirement groups, and nonprofit organizations.

Dan received a Bachelor of Arts degree in Economics from Stanford University and a Master of Business Administration degree from the Walter A. Haas School of Business, University of California at Berkeley. He is a Chartered Financial Analyst (CFA), Certified Financial Planner (CFP), and registered securities representative of Reinhardt Werba Bowen Securities, Inc., a registered NASD broker/dealer. He is also a member of the Institute of Chartered Financial Analysts, the Association of Investment Management and Research, and the Security Analysts of San Francisco.

Prior to joining Reinhardt Werba Bowen Advisory Services, Dan competed on the men's professional tennis tour and was a Wimbledon quarterfinalist and the 27th best player in the world. As an undergraduate, he received Stanford University's PAC-10 Student Athlete Award and won the 1986 NCAA Singles Championship in Men's Tennis.